You Know I Love You Because You're Still Alive

Confessions of a Middle Aged Working Mom

Lori B. Duff

You Know I Love You Because You're Still Alive

CONFESSIONS OF A MIDDLE AGED WORKING MOM

Dear Kim –
Don't be Fawn Hall!
You rock!
Lori B Duff

Lori B Duff

This book is mostly a work of non-fiction. Memory is a strange thing, and no two people's recollections of things are the same. This is what happened as I remember it, or as I recreate it because the truth wasn't quite as funny without being tweaked. If I tease you in here, it's because I love you. You know it because you're still alive.

ISBN: 9780692775653
ISBN10: 069277565X

Lori B. Duff follows up *Mismatched Shoes and Upside Down Pizza* and *The Armadillo, the Pickaxe, and the Laundry Basket* with her third hilarious collection of essays

Here's what people are saying:

"Lori Duff fully admits to having a high tolerance for shenanigans and an inability to feel shame while making a fool of herself. Those traits combine to make a hilarious, and sometimes tender, book full of stories about a modern mother and her ever-challenging life. Whether she is experiencing Pinterest fails while baking or daydreaming of bombarding coworkers who arrive late with a paintball gun full of Sharpie ink, Lori's quick wit and charm will definitely win you over." – Keith Stewart, author of *Bernadette Peters Hates Me*

"Take a peek inside Lori Duff's hectic but happy life and realize you're not alone in trying to balance work, family, marriage and home. With hilarious anecdotes and brutal honesty, she finishes her legal work while making chicken soup and leaves to chaperone a student trip to the Hotel of Doom. Laughing with Lori could become a welcome habit." – Elaine Ambrose, author of *Midlife Cabernet* and *Midlife Happy Hour*

"About halfway through this book I realized that Lori Duff is saying a lot of smart and true and salient things WHILE she's making me laugh out loud until my stomach hurts." – Mary Patterson Thornburg, author of *The Kura* and *A Glimmer of Guile*

"If Erma Bombeck and Andy Rooney had a secret love child and she grew up to be a writer, it would be Lori Duff. Enjoy this funny, sweet, ironic collection of essays." --Heather J. McAdams, author of *Desolation Sound*

"Duff embraces her middle-aged, working-mom role with gusto and Erma Bombeck-esque humor in her latest sidesplitter, a page turner that'll have you shaking your head in agreement one minute; laughing your head off the next." – Allia Zobel Nolan, author of *Women Who Still Love Cats Too Much*

"Lori Duff's essays get to the point quickly, proclaiming that "Some people will do anything to get out of volunteering" and "There's a reason ….She speaks for many other working middle-aged moms who "only want to be left alone" and are certainly "too old for overtime." Duff's book is heartfelt, laugh-out-loud funny and ends with this sage advice: "Forgiving is healthy. Forgetting is for fools." – Gianetta Palmer, author of *Reflections on a Middle Aged Fat Woman*

"Whether she's inventing hysterical television game shows for couples, creating witty public service announcements, drafting the new Bill of Parents' Rights, or imparting her famous chicken soup recipe in amusing narrative form, Lori Duff's uproarious voice-of-reason will resonate long after you've read her cover-to-cover. With perfectly seasoned chapters and a tone that's anything but mild, she's got just the right amount of spiciness to inscribe clever sayings on Taco Bell hot sauce packets. Lucky for us, Ms. Duff prefers to write books. And hilarious ones at that!" – Stephanie D. Lewis, author of *Lullabies & Alibis*

Table of Contents

This Book is Dedicated To
Everyone I Love Enough Not to Murder in Their Sleep.

I guess that's all y'all.

You Know I Love
You Because
You're Still Alive

You Know I Love You Because You're Still Alive

Chaperoning at the Crack Smoking Hotel

I am chaperoning a Middle School Band festival. Yes, I know. Living the dream.

Seriously, it is a thing I am happy to do, and I took off a day of work just to do it. I think it is fantastic that there are this many young teenagers who are into the arts and wear their self-proclaimed band geekiness as proudly as they would a letter jacket. They are me thirty- some-odd years ago. I was looking forward to it. There was to be music, bonding time with my son and his friends, and I was promised that all I had to do was transport the kids from point A to point B and the rest of the time was mine. What could be bad? I brought work with me. I listed ideas for articles and blog posts hopefully in a purple three ring binder. I brought two books, in case I finished the first one. These things happen, you know, and one must be prepared.

The festival is in Athens, which is the home of the University of Georgia. It is a great college town, funky and fun, and less than an hour's drive from my house. Because there are late nights and early mornings, we are staying in a hotel. There are seven kids, only four of whom (including my own) I have met before this trip; one band director, who is quite literally half my age and one third my size; and another mother, who is about my age, and, well, my kind of person, only I didn't know that before I got here. I wish I had. Things would have been different. There was supposed to be one more parent, but she had emergency surgery a few days before the festival, and her surgeon forbade her participation. Some people will do anything to get out of volunteering.

After the first afternoon's festivities and evening concert, we went to check in the hotel. It wasn't one I was familiar with, but I'm not familiar with many hotels in Athens. Seeing as how the band director graduated from UGA about twenty minutes ago, I figured she knew where/what it was and I wasn't worried. Most chain hotels have a certain standard, and I'm not that terribly picky.

I piled my son, two other boys, and a girl in my car, and we headed to the hotel with directions from the GPS. We drove by it the first time, even though the GPS was yelling at me that we had reached our destination. I guess I refused to see what was plainly in front of me. We pulled in a parking lot, and the girl asked Siri where our hotel was. Siri gave us directions back to where we had been. Well, I thought, maybe we missed it. We turned around and drove by again, this time with the children and Siri yelling at me, and the kids adding that they were pretty sure they saw Gabby's mother's car.

I pulled in to a place that might have been a television set from a police drama. The lobby, once you got past the Plexiglas window with the speaker, roundhouse kicked you in the face with the odor of stale cigarettes. Our seven little country kids, sheltered in their upper middle class residential neighborhood, had never seen such a thing. They were visibly shaking.

I wish I could say the rooms were better than the lobby suggested. We took three flights of crooked concrete stairs up to a sloped landing, trying not to kick over an anthill of cigarette butts. The two girls I was in charge of and I shouldered our door open.

The heat hit me first. It was a living, breathing thing: thick and viscous. The 'climate control' unit was not running, but it was set on 'heat.' Or maybe 'inferno,' or maybe 'autoclave.' I turned it on "air conditioning" and set the temperature on 68. I'm not sure that ever did anything, but at least I felt like I was trying.

I wanted to cry. I didn't want to freak out the girls, so I kept a smile plastered on my face. I didn't want to seem like a snob, so I said nothing to the other mother or the teacher. I know I've gotten soft in my old age, and my income allows me to avoid certain discomforts and hold to certain standards. The toilet seemed relatively clean, despite what we decided (for sanity's sake) were 'rust' stains at the bottom of the drain. The edges of the bathroom floor were crusted with mold and dark patches and fuzzy stuff that might or might not have once been hair. I didn't look too closely. The beds seemed cleanish, if you ignored the cigarette burns in the bedding and the eau-de-unfiltered-Camel in the pillows. I've been primitive camping, and I can tell you there are fewer bugs and less dirt on the side of a mountain.

I didn't know what to do. I really didn't. I was in charge of my two girls and the three boys in the room next door, all of us on the third floor. It was late at night and we were exhausted. I went to check on the boys. They were boys. They were making fun of the condition of the hotel, but didn't seem disturbed by it.

I went back to the girls' room. I stood in the middle of the room, unsure of what to do. The girls had plopped themselves on the bed to do some homework, and the boys, in their room, were watching television. I didn't even want to let my socks touch the carpet, much less expose any unnecessary flesh to the elements and risk being attacked by a swarm of cooties while I put my pajamas on, so I stood there for a while in a kind of stunned silence.

I decided to make the best of it. I looked up the motel on line to see if there were any reviews of it. When I clicked on the TripAdvisor reviews, the very first said, "Crack Smoking Hotel of Choice in the Athens Area." I started to laugh and couldn't stop. The girls looked over my shoulder and began to read and laugh themselves. The best part about a college town is that the people in it tend to be articulate, and these reviews, speaking of the aura of despair surrounding the motel, were written by folks who have read a lot of dramatic fiction. Most of the reviews were written by people in town for a football game who couldn't find lodging anywhere else. About half of them elected to sleep in their cars instead. The only positive review was from one woman who seemed thrilled that the hotel allowed her to bring in her cat. Which, now that I think of it, might explain that odd smell in the corner of the room and the paw print on my son's pillowcase.

I was truly at a loss. I texted the other Mom (whose name at that point I honestly still did not know) and went out on a limb – "I think we should change hotels tomorrow night." I didn't hear back. I did not insist that anyone take a shower or brush their teeth or do anything that would require using the facilities we were given.

Eventually, I put on my pajamas and gingerly got into bed, trying as hard as I could not to sink too deeply into the mattress along with whatever substances over the years had also sunk deeply into the mattress. I curled into the fetal position, and lay there for about six hours with my eyes wide open. I think the girls slept. They were quiet and breathing deeply, anyway.

In the wee hours of the morning I got up. I tried to wash my face, but there were no towels. No bath towels at all: one washcloth and a hand towel. The washcloth had makeup all over it. I made an executive decision. If I had to pay for all four rooms, I was going to get us in a nicer hotel. I checked online for availability at the Holiday Inn.

I sent a text message to the other Mom (who I was still forced to think of as "Gabby's Mom" since the girls didn't know her first name either, and her last name is virtually unpronounceable, but whose number

I had from group texts from the band director) telling her of my decision and asking her if she wanted to go in on it with me. She instantly agreed. I then sent a message to the band director who was skeptical that rooms would be available. I called the hotel, reserved four rooms within 90 seconds, got email confirmation, and let her know we were moving.

I banged on the boys' door. "Time to get up! And pack your stuff. We're moving to the Holiday Inn." I spent a while soaking up the praise for my wisdom and general all around awesomeness I would have killed for when I was 13 from teenage boys.

Theoretically, the crack motel had a complimentary continental breakfast. I checked it out before I let any of the kids eat. There were some pre-wrapped muffins made in an industrial bakery somewhere else, boxes of cereal, and bananas with thick, unbroken peels. So we got breakfast. The milk was only two days gone, but it was good enough for the coffee served in individually wrapped-at-the-factory cups. It didn't curdle, and there was caffeine in the coffee. That's all I needed on a short term basis.

After we got the kids settled in their rehearsals, Eleni (the other Mom: I found out her name from one of the girls who asked her daughter) and I, who had since bonded over our shared horror, went to the Holiday Inn together to check in and bring up the luggage. "Welcome to Holiday Inn," the fresh faced, well-scrubbed desk clerk sang out to us. There was nothing between him and us, no bullet-proof Plexiglas, and no ashy haze of smoke. Just clean, air conditioned air, with a faint smell of recently used cleaning products.

"You have no idea how happy I am to be here." I said. "I have never in my life been so happy to be anywhere. Thank you so much for letting us stay here." I thought about leaping over the counter and kissing the young man on his clean-shaven face. The clerk looked at me sideways, no doubt wondering what kind of crazy person was so excited to stay at a Holiday Inn in a decidedly non-exotic location, but otherwise took my exuberance in stride. He and the other clerk efficiently got us keys for two sets of adjoining rooms. We checked in our respective rooms and each took long, hot showers guaranteed to kill any lingering cooties. Clean and settled in, we went about our chaperoning duties with a great deal more enthusiasm.

I have to say, these are truly great kids. They took their adventure in stride, laughed about it heartily, and went on to play beautiful music. They are fortunate to have the opportunity, and to have a teacher who takes her personal time to make sure it happens for them. I'd do it again in a minute. As long as I get to make the hotel reservations.

The Post-Newlywed Game

Recently, my husband and I have had the 5,263,276th petty squabble of our marriage regarding what exactly happened in some non-event in the recent past. We argue like this a lot. "No. That's not what she said." "No, we had the steak." "Um, no, it was the *Batman* ride at Six Flags that I threw up on."

These are stupid arguments. But I'm positive I'm right. Mike is just as convinced. One of us has to be wrong. (It's him.) In continuing legal education, I've been involved in any number of trial technique classes that demonstrate how unreliable eye witnesses can be. Sometimes there will be a guy who comes in and surreptitiously takes someone's jacket, and then fifteen minutes later there is a quiz about the guy. No one remembers him the same way. Same goes for the witnesses in a car accident. The blue car ran the red light. No, the yellow one. It was a Ford. It was a Chevy. It was a Lamborghini. It was an SUV. It was a minivan. No one agrees.

Least of all spouses like us who are so far beyond the newlywed stages that pre-marriage life is kind of faded and grey; the memories more like a ghost of a film I've seen decades ago than something that has actually happened to me.

All of which is a very long introduction to this fabulous idea I just had. Pay attention Merv Griffin or Mark Burnett or whoever is in charge of game shows these days. This show is going to be Must See TV. It is going to make "Survivor" look like a day at Chuck-E-Cheese. It will make "Jeopardy!" look as challenging as the TV Guide crossword puzzle.

Picture this: you get your basic couple, and follow them around on a random Saturday. Nothing exciting needs to happen, but it all gets filmed. They go to the grocery store. They take the kids to a soccer game. Someone mows the lawn. Nothing you would normally consider television worthy happens, but plenty of stuff happens. A referee makes a bad call, someone does something stupid in traffic, you buy the lean or the cheap ground beef, or one of your kids spills his milk.

Then the show opens. The couple is sitting on a sofa. The host is in an armchair. It looks sort of like a talk show. The host says something like, "So, Bob, Mary, I understand you went to your daughter's gymnastics meet last week." Bob and Mary nod, though their names are actually Steve and Dina, but they don't want to embarrass the host on national television. "Which one of you forgot the camera?" Bob and Mary start arguing. Normally Bob brings the camera, but he has a very clear memory of telling Mary to grab it off the kitchen counter. Mary heard no such thing. Cut to the film. We see Mary in the kitchen washing the breakfast dishes. Bob says, "Hon? My hands are full. Can you get the camera? It is on the shelf in the office." Mary makes a noise that sounds like, "Mmph" and Bob says "Thanks." Score one for Bob.

The host then says, "Our cameras showed you all looking for the remote control for the living room television. It was found on the kitchen counter next to the cookie jar. Who put it there?"

"I know this one," Bob says. "Our daughter, Emily, is always stealing cookies out of the jar and moving the remote."

"It wasn't Emily," Mary says. "It was you. You carry that thing all over the house and then blame everyone else when it gets lost."

"No," Bob says. "I always put it back on the coffee table where it belongs because I'm tired of looking for the thing."

The host rolls the film. It shows Bob going into the kitchen, laying the remote down on the counter, and cramming a fistful of Oreos in his mouth. Score one for Mary.

I would watch that show like it held the secrets to the universe. I would also watch the follow up show where the couples are revisited six months later. It would be interesting to see how many are still married.

I would never be on that show, though. I prefer the sure knowledge that I'm always right. If only my husband would buy into that as well.

Becoming a Man

Author's Note:

On Saturday, October 25, 2014, my son became a Bar Mitzvah. It is traditional for the Bar Mitzvah boy's parents to say nice things about him to the whole congregation. Following is my speech from my son Jacob's Bar Mitzvah.

Normally, it is bad form to brag about your kids to a captive audience. But today isn't normal, so I'm going to take advantage of my position as the person who is feeding you lunch to tell you what an amazing son I have.

This kid has always been precocious. He walked early, he talked early: he was even born early. He's always had this engaging charm. When he was a baby he would seek people out and stick his little hand towards them like he was running for Mayor of Babyville. He picked up his first woman in a bar when he was only nine months old, while we were waiting on a table at a restaurant on Jekyll Island and he leaped out of my arms into those of a buxom blonde who caught his eye.

And here we are. He's gone from being a six and a half pound peanut who was allergic to every food under the sun to being this – this healthy, brilliant, talented man-child who is taller than I am when I'm not wearing heels. I have no idea how it happened.

What can I say? What can I say about a kid who spontaneously says things like, "I can't stand the kitchen anymore, I'm going to clean it?" What can I say about a kid who, since he was tall enough to pour water in the carafe, will make coffee in the morning and bring it to me in bed? What can I say about a boy who gets himself ready for school in the morning, who always does his homework, who always gets A's on his report cards, and who never not once has gotten in trouble at school? Except that one time when he said a bad word after getting out in the spelling bee. And to his credit he used it properly and in context and had no idea it was a bad word and told the teacher he learned it "when Mommy spilled the pink drink in the car." The only thing I can think to say about him is this: all you mothers out there, the dowry wars have already begun. Feel free to jump right in and make the field that much more competitive.

There has been so much work leading up until today. Meryl Romeu worked with him as his Bar Mitzvah mentor. Rabbi Kirzner had to give him that 'look' a few times. I gave him an awful lot of grief myself, probably more than he deserved. He started his education here at Temple Beth David at the ripe old age of three at Tot Shabbat. Then came Sunday school classes, and five years' worth of Hebrew School, then confirmation classes and youth group. He did all of this not only without complaint, but with true regret if we couldn't make it one time or another. In fact, I'm sure Mike and I complained more about hauling him into Snellville so often than he did about the additional school he was being hauled to. If you don't speak Yiddish, and you want to know what a *mensch* is, you need look no further than my son.

I wish I could take credit for him. But aside from not contributing any genetic material to mess it all up, I can't say I did anything to make him be this wonderful creature that he is. He is so self-motivated. He drives himself hard and cuts himself no slack. If I had let him be raised by the coyotes that we sometimes hear yowling creepily in our back yard, he probably would have turned out just as well. Maybe not as well read or as good at playing the saxophone and oboe, and maybe not as concerned with personal hygiene, and certainly not addicted to Dr. Who, but his character and heart would have been the same. He'd have been the alpha coyote as soon as he was weaned. He's that naturally good, and naturally a leader. In only seventh grade, he is president of the Loganville Middle School Council. He starred in the Temple Beth David Youth Group's production of Joseph and the Amazing Technicolor Dreamcoat, and now he's an officer in the Youth Group. He can't imagine sitting back and letting things drift by him. He's always in the thick of it, my sweet boy.

I guess after today I should say my sweet man. Today, bubelah, you become a man. Which means that tomorrow, you need to get a job. Just kidding. And you still can't drive my car for another three years. Seriously, today is supposed to be the day that you take on the responsibility of your own education and obligations as a member of the Jewish community. But you're not going to do that today. I know you're not.

Because you already did it years ago, without even being asked.

I love you Jacob. You are the best boy in the whole entire world.

When Mummy Gets Sick

I have no time to get sick. I don't know about you, but there are only 24 hours in my day. Laundry doesn't fold itself, phone calls don't make themselves, paperwork doesn't do itself and file itself, and children of all ages need hand holding and encouragement and comforting. It is not on most Moms' list of options to get anything more dicey than the sniffles.

And yet we are humans, and it happens. A week and change ago was my son's Bar Mitzvah. (Or, as we call it around here, the Big BM.) The weekend before was another friend had a Big BM of his own, and in addition to the normal public contact I have, I spent the weekend in close quarters with good friends. Including the friends of my children, wonderful, affectionate, well-behaved little germ factories that they are.

I guess because of my high tolerance for shenanigans and my inability to feel shame of any kind while making a fool of myself, my children's friends seem to like me. So, when Jacob's friend Annie started a trend called "nose cuddling" I went along for the ride. Annie rubs the tip of her nose against my cheek and when she is finished, gives me a little blast of nose air. It sounds grosser typed out than it actually is. No boogers are exchanged in the transaction, even if there are fifty billion airborne pathogens. It is affectionate, and cute, and intimate, and it feels much like a cat scenting me. Often, Annie and Jacob will get me on either side and double nose cuddle me. Their mutual friend Ali will join in, together or separately, now that it has been established as a 'thing.' [And here, for reasons beknownst only to me and Annie, I am contractually obligated to make the following statement: Annie gives the best nose cuddles.] The other Moms thought I was nuts. I thought it was a parenting win.

So anyway, I got a lot of nose cuddles from Ali and Annie and Jacob the weekend before the Big BM. On Monday, Ali announced her diagnosis with strep throat. Fab-u-licious! We sat back and did everything we could to make sure that the other shoe would not drop. After all, Jacob had to sing in Hebrew for the better part of two hours in front of a crowd of a hundred fifty friends and relatives, and we both had to give speeches. Getting sick was NOT an option. We took vitamin C. We drank orange juice. We made matzoh ball soup (and, I need to remind you, I am an authentic, purebred Jewish mother, so I know how to make chicken soup. If you're lucky, I will share my secrets with you later.) We went to bed early. We both got the sniffles, but no fevers and nothing strep-y. We each got through the day in question without health being an issue.

And then it was over. For months, I had slept, ate, breathed, and thought about precious little else than the Big BM. On Sunday, when we came home from the hotel and kissed the last of family goodbye and unloaded everything from the car, I felt the magnetic pull of my own mattress and crashed face first with my makeup, jewelry, and shoes still on and I didn't get up for another four hours.

Since then, it has been down hill in the health department. I have gotten steadily sicker. I allowed myself to sleep in on Monday, not that it did me any good. I ate soup, drank Dayquil and Nyquil, I neti-potted my sinuses, I rested when I could. Nothing made me feel better. My breath, as my daughter so dramatically put it, "smelled like Ebola." Still, I soldiered on, because really, what choice did I have?

Not much of one. I had promised to help out Ali's Mom with all the food and clean up for Ali's Bat Mitzvah, the weekend after my son's. I pride myself on being reliable. If I say I'm gonna do something, I'm gonna do it, no matter how much plague I spread. I washed my hands raw and dramatically often to avoid spreading whatever I had. I kept hoping that someone would say, "You look terrible. Why don't you sit down and don't even breathe near the food." But no one did. So I soldiered on, doing a fantastically lousy job. The simple task of laying brownies out on a plate was beyond my capabilities.

By the time the service was over, the luncheon was served and put away, and the party began, I was completely wiped. But Ali, who I am here contractually obligated to say "will always be my favorite" is worth pushing through. My plan was to sit, eat my catered food, and let the party drift by me.

Then the DJ played "Brick House." I had to rally for that one, and waggle my Brick House of a back side along with a group of about six other middle aged women. I sat back down and took a nap. To the outside observer, I was sitting quietly minding my own business. In reality, I was wandering around the cobwebby nether regions of my brain, completely somewhere else. I was vaguely aware of the DJ playing games with the kids, and trying to get grownups to participate. And then, despite the fact that there were approximately 100 other people over the age of 18 in the room, somehow I found myself being dragged out of my chair and wrapped in toilet paper like a mummy, stuck with stickers, and marked upon. I was actually happy when they wrapped toilet paper over my head and blocked my vision. I closed my eyes and checked out for a moment more, standing in the middle of the dance floor. Pictures were taken. I was thanked for being a good sport.

In the car on the way home, I laid my head against the window, fantasized about my bed and sleeping in the next day, and asked my children why I had to be picked. "Because," my daughter said. "Everyone likes you. You're a cool Mom."

And that, my friends, made me feel much, much better.

The Hoodie

We had been shopping at the Outlet Mall earlier in the day, and my unsupervised husband, Mike, found himself alone in American Eagle. Apparently he forgot that he is approximately forty years too old to shop in that store. He bought himself a clearance hoodie, complete with the logo emblazoned on the front, and wore it the rest of the day, much to the abject horror of the teenagers living in my home.

He was still wearing the hoodie when he went down into the basement to fill up the base of a freestanding punching bag with water for my daughter to both practice her karate and release her frustrations that she is stuck living with the most ridiculous parents and brother on the planet. To hear her say it, anyway.

There was some old, grody water left over in the base of the punching bag stand, and Mike dragged it over to the basement door and tipped it to let it out in the grass. Something tipped a little too far, and his feet found themselves north of his hips. He managed to fall in the grass instead of the concrete floor in the basement, and the only injuries were to pride and the American Eagle hoodie, which ended up covered in mud.

By this time it was about 11 at night, the time at which I am floating off to enjoy one of my three recurring dreams, and Mike gets his one and only burst of energy for the day. I was just about to finish a chapter in my book and put it to the side when I heard a loud flurry of words I wish my children didn't hear. I said a quiet little prayer that they had snuck their iPods into their room and were listening to whoever the band du jour was through their earbuds.

"Are you ok?" I shouted, warm under the flannel sheets and hoping to not have to get out and ruin the body heated pocket of snuggliness I created under the covers.

"Yeah," said my husband, and I turned back to my book. Not two minutes later he said, "Lori! Please! It's an emergency!"

I flung aside the covers and braved the cold to see what was the matter. Before I got down the hallway I heard, "I flooded the laundry room. I need you to go in the basement and see if the water is coming through the ceiling."

I ran back to my room to get house shoes and went into the basement, followed rather quickly by my son, who wasn't smart enough to put on shoes first. I could hear it before I saw it, the waterfall coming through the floor, across the joists, collecting on the pipes and dripping on to the random detritus in the basement.

That's the thing about my basement. You can't just assume anything. There might be a bag of trash sitting on top of a suitcase full of tax returns; in a container that seems like it is full of junk mail and old phone books, there might also be a car title. This happens because my husband has a tendency to 'clean' by sweeping out-of-place things into a bag or box and then hiding the bag or box in the basement, never to be touched again. So you need to be careful. Underneath the deluge was a pile of boxes and bags that could have been filed with the original Magna Carta, Chinese take-out menus from restaurants that are no longer in business, savings bonds, mouse turds, and somebody's will. It was important to rescue them all.

I found an old cat litter bucket (we haven't had a cat since 2002) and put it underneath the majority of the rainfall, and my son and I began moving boxes and bags into the dry zone. Mike flung some old towels down the basement steps, and I mopped up as best I could. Mike took a break from mopping the laundry room to see the damage downstairs.

We swapped places then, and I took on the mopping duties in the laundry room. My son stood outside the laundry room trying to gauge my mood. "This is funny, right?"

"It will be tomorrow," I said.

It didn't take too long to soak up and relocate enough water that it was no longer pouring through the floor. Mike and I took a break from mopping and hauling and I asked the Sixty-Four Thousand Dollar question: how exactly did he flood the laundry room?

It was all the hoodie's fault. There was mud on the new hoodie, and this Would Not Do. Since it was new, Mike actually read the laundry care label, and learned he should wash it on cold. Before he did that, however, he wanted to rinse the mud off. So he put it in the laundry sink and turned on the water. And walked away. And forgot the water was on.

Jacob tried to convince Mike that this was God, or karma, or the universe, or whoever is in charge of such things, telling Mike that wearing an American Eagle hoodie designed for a 15 year old when you are old enough to get the senior discount at the grocery store is a terrible idea.

"I like that sweatshirt," Mike said, refusing to call it a hoodie. "It's comfortable and it fits."

Jacob just shook his head. It's an old cliché for a reason: you really can't teach an old dog new tricks. Or much of anything else, either.

Becoming Boxless

There are two basic ways in which brains are wired in the Duff household. One way is the way my son and I think of the universe. Jacob and I? We like the box. We find the walls of the box comforting. We like rules and lists and limits and structure. There are plenty of toys to play with inside of the box, and plenty of creative things you can do with the tools you find there. Neither of us can understand why you'd play a game any way but by the rules. Where's the challenge in that?

Then there is the boxless faction, my husband and daughter. Marin is only vaguely aware that there is a box. While her moral compass generally points north, and she is a pretty well behaved kid, and even insists on the rules of proper grammar, this is because she has determined by her own observation and conclusions that this is the way things should be, and not because of some set of rules or expectations imposed by anyone else.

Neither one of these essential natures is a better way to be. This is good, because due to the hard wiring of our brains, I doubt there is a pill or program or system that could change any of us or even modify us all that much.

I worry, naturally, that Marin's completely different way of approaching the world on her own terms will result in disaster, because such a thing would never even occur to me. Sometimes I want to get on her about it, but often, that's where her greatest successes come from.

Take the assignment she had in her language arts class. (An aside: why oh why oh why can't this be called 'English' class like in the olden days?) She was supposed to write an essay about her favorite teacher, and why she chose this particular teacher. Being eleven, and therefore smarter and more knowledgeable than any adult she ever came into contact with, she refused to acknowledge that any of her teachers had taught her anything even remotely worthwhile. I listed all the teachers she'd loved over the years, and she said no. I listed her Sunday School and Hebrew

School teachers. Also rejected. I suggested her father or me, or maybe her grandparents. Nope, nope, and nope. She finally settled on the band "Five Seconds of Summer," also known as 5SOS, which she believed at the time was the answer to life, the universe, and everything. Their lyrics, she declared, taught her everything she needed to know about life. This idea was soundly (and righteously) rejected by her teacher.

So needless to say, after weeks of flat out refusing to follow the rules, there came a time when the essay was due in ten minutes. She grabbed a piece of notebook paper, scribbled down what popped into her head, and turned it in.

Later, I found out that her off-the-cuff essay was deemed of a sufficient quality that she was to be one of only two students to read theirs at the 5th grade awards night. I hadn't read it – all I knew is that she settled on "life" being her teacher, and I was more than a little miffed that her 11 year old equivalent of giving the finger to an assignment reaped praise and reward.

Then came the awards ceremony. The time came on the program for her to read it. Her similarly boxless father had not yet made it to the school, and I fretted that he would miss it. Never fear, however, as Marin is a Duff, and therefore when she got to the podium, everyone discovered that not a soul, not the teacher, not the administrators, and not Marin herself, had thought to bring a copy of the essay to the podium. She was quickly shuttled to the end of the program while her teacher ducked off to find it.

When the time came for her to read it for realsies, and her father had made it into the room, I was completely blown away. Rather than seem half-hearted, or last minute, or attitude-y, it was brilliant. It was wise, it was witty, and not the least bit snarky. If I weren't familiar with the circumstances of its birth, I would have suspected that she copied it from some valedictory speech she found on the internet.

So I guess we're more alike than I thought. We express ourselves better in writing. We've both found success taking a path that is comfortable for us and unique to us. And then we're not alike, because she can do what I can't. She can take the tools inside the box and run with them and combine them with the freedom of the outdoors and make something brilliant I don't have the capacity for. Out of the mouths of babes really does come the truth, even if that wasn't their goal to begin with.

I love that girl, and I admire the heck out of her, even though for now, and probably for the next 7 years or so, she has a deep seated belief that my sole purpose on this Earth is to think of ways to embarrass her and then execute them in front of the greatest number of people.

I'm sure this chapter will embarrass her. Too bad.

Following is the text of her speech, complete with her spelling errors for authenticity's sake:

So many people have made an impact on my life that it is impossible to truely choose just one. I've decided that life itself is my favorite teacher.

Every time I go outside I feel the crisp air surrounding me, and I feel the soft sunlight wrapping me in a blanket of warmth. This is what teaches me the attire I need. I tend to learn from the small things. I learn happiness when my favorite music soothes my hearing. I learn responsibility when procrastination betrays me, but most of all I learn selflessness when others need me more than I do.

Life helps inspire me with it's little blessings; it gives me confidence when I feel there is nowhere I can go, it gives me strength when I least expect it, and bravery when fear stands in the path of my goals. Sure, life can beat me, and everyone else for that matter, but it's the struggles in life that make us tough enough to go on.

In conclusion, to chose a single person as a special teacher to me would be a lie, for life impacts us in a way that no human can.

You're Late

There are two kinds of people in my house: the late kind and the early kind. I'm the early kind. My husband is the late kind. In fact, my husband is so much the late kind that there are times when he doesn't show up at all. Our children are likewise divided. My son is early, and my daughter is late.

Frankly, I think this is not so much of a preference thing as a moral issue, and I am here to condemn half of my family, and probably a good number of my friends, on this front. When you make someone else wait for you, you are, more or less, holding them hostage. You are saying that they have to stop, waste their time, and do nothing just waiting for you to catch up.

There are so many things you say when you are late. You say, "My sleeping in five minutes more was more important to me than your time." You say, "Making sure my hair looked 'just so' was more important to me than the fact that you were getting aggravated." You say, "Doing things my way merely for the sake of stubbornness is more important to me than your feelings."

You didn't need that drink of water before you left, you wanted it. It isn't like were about to go on a barefoot trek across the Sahara Desert and you don't know when you'll be able to refill the canteen. The worst part is that the late people always win: the early people don't get to force the late people to be early, but the late people force the early people to be late.

This is probably the source of more hard feelings in my family than any other issue. It easily beats "you're hogging the bathroom," "turn down that music," and "you stole my hairbrush/hoodie/box of Thin Mints." And not just between the young 'uns, this is between the grownups, too.

I am of the opinion that if you are going to a meeting that starts at 6, you need to be there at 5:45 so you have time to take off your coat, do a pre-emptive bathroom run, and settle in and say hello before things actually get started. Whenever the lecturer, moderator, or person in charge says something like, "There are still people coming in so we'll wait until everyone gets settled," I wish I had a paintball gun filled with Sharpie ink so that I could pelt the latecomers with indelible shame marks. I got here on time, now I have to be here an extra ten minutes because you couldn't get your act together. Unacceptable. You stole ten minutes of my life. You're a robber.

Ok, that's extreme, I know, but I happen to have extreme feelings on the matter.

This is why parties make me nervous. I mean, aside from the whole "I'm terrible at small talk and hate crowds and people exhaust me" thing. If an invitation says that something starts at 7, then I think it starts at 7. And some things do. But sometimes, 7 actually means 9, or maybe "sometime before midnight." I have no ability whatsoever to figure out which is which. As a result, I am either the first one to arrive, and I make the hostess nervous because she is still in her bathrobe because who comes to a party on time or I get there after the pigs in a blanket have already been eaten and the good conversation topics have already been exhausted.

Of course, if I am going with my family we are guaranteed to be late. There are whole categories of people to whom I no longer even apologize, because I know they know it isn't my fault and they are tired of hearing about it.

It seems an odd thing to have a genetic predisposition to being on time, though I can see it in action in my own family. My daughter doesn't choose to be late: watching her get ready for things is like watching her father get ready for things. They seem physically incapable of doing things linearly. It is kind of like a sense of direction, I think. Some people can just orient themselves and know where they are. Maybe it is an innate sense of knowing where magnetic north is, or maybe it is just an instinct, or maybe some distant ancestor somehow spliced genes with a homing pigeon. Some people can't go three miles in unfamiliar territory without getting lost, even with the assistance of a GPS shouting at them in a vaguely British accent to make a left turn NOW.

Maybe, like a sense of direction, some people have a sense of time. I can feel minutes ticking by. If I know I have thirty minutes to get ready for something, each one of those thirty minutes looms over me. I feel like Dorothy in the Wicked Witch of the West's castle in the Wizard of Oz, knowing that doom will come when the sand runs out of the hourglass. I think people like my husband and daughter are as unaware of the passage of time as they are of the Wi-Fi signals pinging through the house. It's a sensory blindness: something that just happens below their collective radar dishes.

I don't know. But just like a GPS can tell you where to turn if you don't have a sense of direction, a watch can tell you what time it is. Even old school cell phones have timers and reminders on them. Use them. Because being late? Not cool.

Then again, I've never been accused of being cool.

Piercing His Ears

My thirteen year old son wants his ears pierced. My sunny little blonde haired blued eyed smiling little boy wants to poke holes in his head and decorate himself.

Ok, his hair isn't clear yellow anymore: it has become a light brown/ dirty blonde, and he isn't little so much as 5'9", but his eyes are still blue, and he is still sunny and usually smiling.

I have a visceral reaction to this request for earrings, which is a loud, resounding "No, no, no, not in my lifetime, no."

Jacob's arguments are sound, which is a problem for me. I like to have logic on my side, and I'm afraid I don't on this one. His irrefutable arguments are these: 1. He has proven his responsibility. 2. His sister, who is two years younger than him, has had her ears pierced for years. 3. His grades are outstanding and he keeps his room neat and does his own laundry. He has earned this privilege. 4. Earrings on a boy are not alternative or counterculture or rebellious like they were when the Earth was still cooling and I was thirteen. 5. Many boys his age who are generally good boys have pierced ears. 6. Many of my male friends who are perfectly decent human beings in addition to being in their forties or beyond have pierced ears, and they managed to have decent, stable jobs. 7. He can always just take them out and you could barely see the hole, just like I can barely see mine when I am not wearing earrings. 8. He will be 14 in a few weeks, and we can't think of anything better to get him as a present.

My husband says no, for one reason and for one reason only: my son is a guy. Guys don't wear earrings.

Mike is even older than I am.

My Dad, who is even older than that, doesn't even like earrings on women. He says, "If God wanted extra holes in your head, He would have put them there."

I searched deep for the root of my reasoning. If I was honest with myself, I had to admit that a lot of it had to do with public perception.

There are at least four women that I am aware of who are vying to be his future mother in law. This means that they want their daughters to end up with a boy like him. I can think of no higher compliment. This is no doubt because he is smart, good looking, polite, and well-behaved. He looks clean cut and well scrubbed. I fear that earrings will mar this image.

I challenged him to find a picture of a non-celebrity guy who was wearing the type of earrings he wanted to wear who didn't look like a thug. It took him five minutes to find an adorably cute, quirky looking guy with the same coloring and basic look as Jacob and small black dots in his ears. I still didn't care for the fashion, but the earrings were no more a part of my dislike of the outfit than the jacket with a weird collar the guy was wearing.

It comes down to a boy vs. girl thing in my mind, and I am conditioned to think that if I want to say that girls can do anything boys can do (only backwards and in high heels, like Ginger Rogers) then it isn't fair to say that boys can't do anything girls can do. Which is a great theory and all, but we are talking about MY boy here, and letting some chickie at the mall or a guy at a tattoo shop violate the very essence of the Hippocratic Oath – first do no harm. The fact that I have done the same thing, and allowed the same thing to be done to my daughter, is immaterial. Or is it?

So I thought this:

I'll try to take off my Mom Goggles for a minute and see this worthy, independent kid for the individual that he is, and I'll let the Court of Public Opinion have a vote. I posted the question on that greatest of hive minds: Facebook. There was no consensus there.

Eventually, true to my nature, I let logic win. His ears still aren't pierced, but I told him that if he still wanted them done at the end of 8th grade that I would let him get it done as a Middle School graduation present. I hoped he would forget.

I first wrote this chapter in October. It's now May, and we are two weeks away from graduation. He still wants them pierced. The fact that I still feel squishy about it isn't going to make me go back on my word, because my squishy feelings are illogical and I can be Spock-like at times.

Still – I think he needs earrings like he needs holes in his head.

I'm Just
Awkward

I'm Just Awkward

Pedicures

I'm pretty sure there is a zoning ordinance in my area – possibly in the whole state, and possibly in parts beyond – that if you are building a strip mall with more than three store fronts in it, you have to have at least one nail salon and one martial arts studio. You wouldn't think there were enough finger and toe nails and budding ninjas to support these businesses, but wherever you go there are crowds of people.

I don't get my nails done that often, probably less than I should. Being a lawyer, my image matters, and if I have raggedy nails I feel like people will think my work is raggedy. If I am going to wear open toed shoes, I have to have neat, polished toenails.

Pedicures are weird things. Don't get me wrong – I like getting them, and I like the way my toes look without all the funky stuff, and with a neat, clean shape and color. But I can't help but feel funny paying a perfect stranger to sit beneath me as I perch on a giant massaging throne and intimately touch parts of me that my very own children are often too skeeved to be within three feet of. (No pun intended.) I also want to know who exactly came up with the concept that our vestigial claws should be painted bright colors. I mean, at what point between hunting and gathering and our soft, first world lives did we say, "I will not look good without red fingernails!"?

Like nearly every other interaction with strangers that isn't scripted, I never know what to do or say while getting a pedicure. Am I supposed to chit chat with the pedicurist? I'm not there to make friends. I'm there to get the crud scraped out from underneath my toenails and buff my callouses to a nifty sheen. Frankly, I'd rather either close my eyes or read my book. In my experience, most pedicurists don't speak English very well, and although they are always very nice and polite, it seems like they'd rather talk to each other in Korean or Vietnamese, languages which sound to me like bouncing rubber balls tuned to different pitches. I love the sounds. I could listen to it all day. Truly, I don't care if they *are* telling each other about my fat ankles or nasty stuck-in-a-conservative-pump-all-day foot stank. Let them laugh at my lumps and bumps. I don't care. I'm getting my feet rubbed for a reasonable price.

I feel badly sometimes not being able to understand what they are asking me, or not making myself understood. Last week, when I got this done, I wanted to be fancier than normal for my son's Bar Mitzvah. As no detail was left un-obsessed over, I had decided via a committee of friends to get "French' toes with silver tips. I tried to explain this, but didn't get my point across. I got regular 'French' toes with some silver glitter underneath. I decided to make the best of it and got rhinestones across my big toes. The rhinestones were fun for a few days, but now make me feel like a big idiot. Now that I'm not wearing a big, fancy dress and forty-eight pounds of makeup, it just seems like I'm trying to dress up like a four year old. I won't take them off, though. I had fun when I was four.

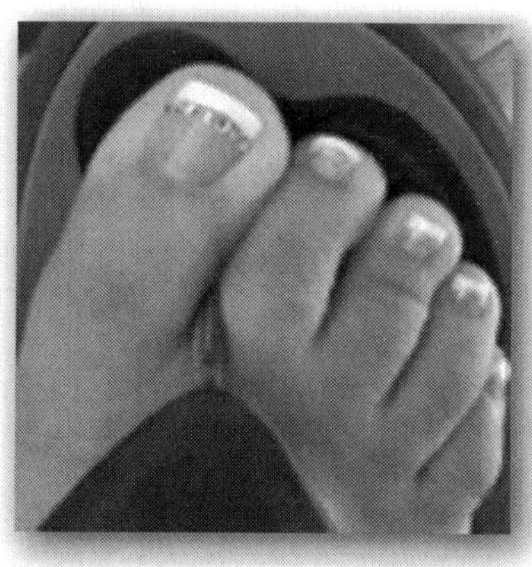

The one thing I don't like is that whenever I get my nails done, the technician seems to be hardwired to want to rip my eyebrows off.

Eyebrow maintenance is, I will grant you, something I don't do often enough, given my natural proclivity to have a single, giant creeping caterpillar across my forehead. But shaped and separated is all I ever want, and what I pay my hairstylist to do. They're still pretty substantial, even after grooming. There's only so much you should fight nature, in my humble opinion. That said, even if I've had them groomed the day before, the nail techs always want to do my eyebrows. I have only let them do it twice before in my life, and both times I ended up looking extremely surprised for a few weeks. No thank you. I prefer to look all knowing. I like my eyebrows wise.

It would be nice, wouldn't it, if we could all start out days with a good rub down, with all extraneous dead skin removed and the feeling that we are all royalty capable of ruling the world? Still, we can't all do that – someone has to actually do the rubbing and the scraping and the pampering. That makes me feel guilty. So I tip well. I think I should pay people well to do the jobs I don't want to do.

And so, if you get nothing else useful from this installment, I hope you at least get this message: the lovely ladies and gentlemen who groom you and hundreds of others every week without making faces or gagging at some of the nasty things they see (and smell) deserve to be well compensated for their time, talent, and discretion. Please, leave a generous tip, look them in the eye, and thank them for making you feel like a star – for a few minutes, anyway. It's the least we can do.

PINTEREST

On the one hand. I don't really like Pinterest very much. It is full of recipe and craft ideas that seem specifically designed to make me feel like a complete and total loser-slash-slacker who has failed her children in every imaginable way. If all the other women out there can somehow manipulate marshmallows and chocolate chips into snowmen, make bento box lunches with fruits and veggies arranged just so in the recognizable shape of Princess Elsa, put up a delicious crockpot meal before heading to work, and get firm abs with only fifteen minutes of exercise a day, why can't I?

So I resent Pinterest. I resent that it holds me up to a standard I don't have a prayer of meeting. I resent that it says that anyone can and should do these things, as if motherhood was some kind of pass or fail competition that depends entirely on your ability and motivation to produce museum quality arts and crafts. Mostly, I resent the word "easy" and the phrase "no time at all." Horsehockey.

And yet I'm drawn to it. I'm drawn to the directions for crochet projects that I'll never make; recipes I'll never try, and memes that were Photoshopped by people who will always have more time (and computer skills) than I have. Pinterest is a time suck, a thing you can get lost in, because the more you click on things, the more it knows what you like, and the more it knows what you like, the more things you truly are interested in pop up.

It irritated me for a long time that I liked it. It irritated me so much I wouldn't even admit that I liked it, instead pretending that I couldn't look away in the way that you can't look away from a horrible wreck on the side of the road. But then last night happened. Last night I had an epiphany. I figured out what I liked about it.

Pinterest is full of hope and humor. Pinterest makes you laugh. Pinterest likes the books and movies and tv shows you like. Pinterest doesn't laugh at you for thinking grammar jokes are funny or for dreaming that you'd still look good in a sparkly tulle skirt. Pinterest believes in a world in which making your own prom dress is not only possible but a good idea.

No one rants about politics on Pinterest. No one tells you that you are some version of idiot because of your political leanings. No one tells you that your form of worship ensures you a first row seat in Hell. Pinterest doesn't force you to look at pictures of cute cats (unless you want to look at cute cats, in which case there is an endless supply of cute cats) and it doesn't brag about other people's children. Nope, you see what you want to see. The more funny stuff you look at, the more funny stuff it gives you. The more pictures of baby sloths you post, the more pictures of baby sloths you see. Lego birthday party ideas? In spades! Want to know how to make a facial mask out of an avocado? Done! Clever jokes about Dr. Who? Gotcha covered. Pinterest is pages and pages of people telling you what they *like,* not what they don't like.

Besides, I'm not convinced that any real actual people do any of those things. Most of the posts were generated by professionals who are hawking a website or book and who create this kind of thing for a living. Or nineteen year olds who really don't have anything better to do with their time than come up with and create clever memes. Or people with money dripping out of their eyeballs so that the nanny or maid or personal assistant does all the scut work and you have nothing but time to individually cut complicated cookies out of refrigerated dough made with hand churned butter derived from cows who get massages twice a week and who only eat organic kale served out of buckets made by women in third world countries who are paid a living wage for their labor. Or something like that.

The rest of us? Just like we read fairy tales and watch implausible romantic comedies, we like living in fantasy worlds, if only for a few minutes at a time. A world in which everyone shares our sense of humor and our taste in clothing and food; and no one ever yells at or belittles anyone.

So yeah. I do like pretending for 12 seconds at a time that there is a prayer I will make that adorable knitted fox hat for my daughter, even though in real life I'm hard pressed to make it to Big Box R Us to buy a cheap serviceable hat for her before the cold weather hits.

A girl can dream, right?

I'm Afraid of the Library

I'm afraid to go back to the library.

I love the library. Any place that is hushed and full of books is by definition magical. I'm jealous of the people who get to work there. No one yells at anyone in a library. Libraries have that awesome paper and binding-glue smell. Librarians get first dibs on new books. (This might not be true, but in my universe, they will have read all the new books as a job requirement so you can ask them if they are any good before you bother checking them out.)

I don't often check out books from the library because I have a book buying problem. As an author, I know how important each individual sale can be. As a reader, I find nothing more comfortable than to be surrounded by stories. Next to my bed is a mound of books waiting to tell me a tale. If I live to 147 I won't have time to read them all, because for each one I read, two more fill its place.

Mostly I go to the library to get books on tape, which aren't on tape anymore, but I'm not sure what I'm supposed to call them and I'm old and set in my ways. Audiobooks, maybe? Anyhoo, since I'm clearly not going to live long enough to read every book on the planet, audiobooks let me squeeze a few more in while I'm driving. They also make the time-wasting frustration of taking forever to get from point "A" to point "B" more productive and enjoyable.

Sometimes, though, I can't help myself. The call of all those shelves of books is too loud to ignore. I look at the spines, waiting for something to catch my eye. I look up my favorite authors to see if maybe I missed something. I look at the new books to see what just came out.

A few weeks ago, probably over two months by now, I checked out InterWorld by Neil Gaiman, one of my favorite authors, and Michael Reaves, a guy I'd never heard of. I read it. I liked it. I gave it to my son to read, and when he finished, I gave it to my husband to read. In the meantime, I went back to the library, renewed InterWorld and checked out The Silver Dream, which was the second in the series. I finished that, and added it to the pile of books on my husband's night table, since he was reading the latest from Christopher Moore, The Serpent of Venice, which I had also checked out from the library and read and passed on. (I almost squealed when I saw it on the new books shelf – that's the kind of book nerd I am proud to be.)

I renewed. And renewed. And returned and checked out new audiobooks. Then I was out of renewals. So I told my husband, "too bad so sad, if you want to read it you have to return InterWorld and check it out with your card." Only he couldn't find it. Somehow it managed to slither of his nightstand and disappear to parts unknown. This was a good week and a half ago. It still hasn't turned up.

So now I'm afraid to go to the library. I have one audiobook in my car that is overdue, and I need to return it, but I can't help but thinking I'm almost done and then I can return it in the middle of the night in the drop box like the criminal I am. I wish I could listen faster so I could just get it done.

I can't bear the disappointed looks I know I will get from the librarians who know me by name even before I present my library card. I can't gird my loins to go in and admit that I was so irresponsible with a book they let me have just on faith that I not only haven't returned it, but can't. I imagine that if I ever try to check out another book some screen with large red letters will pop up on the computer saying something like "CAUTION: IRRESPONSIBLE BOOK BORROWER. USE CARE BEFORE LENDING BOOKS. YOU MIGHT NOT GET THEM BACK."

I know I'm projecting. I'm not the first person to have been responsible for lost a book, nor will I be the last. I will eventually pay my fine, pay for the missing book, and my library card will not be revoked. Still. I wish there were some kind of "first offender" status I could apply for so that it will be wiped off my record. And mostly I'm sad that no one else will be able to read the book I lost.

But really, I'm not the one who lost it. I gave it to my husband's care and HE lost it. Maybe I'll make him go with me and fess up. That's it. I'll pass the buck. But I will no longer pass the book.

Epilogue: After I wrote this, I renewed (ha ha!) my fury at my husband for losing the book. After crawling around on his hands and knees next to the bed and eventually using one of those long sticks with a grabber thing at the end, he managed to retrieve InterWorld from behind the bed. I made him go to the library and return it and explain himself.

Sit or Squat

One of the great joys of being a parent is the chance to drive to East Bumblefudge on your weekend to watch your children participate in whatever sporting/academic/competitive event is going on that Saturday. This past weekend my daughter had an archery tournament in a location a little over two hours from our home.

We were supposed to be there at 9:30 in the morning. Given our inability to function like humans in the morning, least of all a Saturday morning, we decided it was worth our time and money to stay in a hotel the night before. We made a decision to stay in the raving metropolis of Dublin, Georgia, which I have been to before, mainly because it is the only place to stop along I-16 between Savannah and Macon if you have to go potty and/or really need a McDonald's french fry.

After a brief marital spat about which of the myriad of ways to go and what traffic would be like and THIS is why I wanted to leave the house earlier, we decided to take back roads to Dublin on Friday night. I was driving. Our GPS told us it was two hours and fifteen minutes to the hotel. I made everyone go teetee before we left the house, and figured we could do it all in one shot. Only as it turned out, my son and I had made a Starbucks run after I picked him up from the middle school, and about halfway there, we both had a lot of coffee in our systems that was itching to be recycled. I told him I'd stop at the next promising gas station. We saw a non-promising gas station slash bait shop slash serial killer breeding ground, and decided we could wait.

That was a mistake. From that point forwards, there simply was no other bathroom, promising or otherwise, and the situation became more and more critical. It being night, and us being in the absolute epicenter of nowhere, I would have pulled over on the side of the road to allow my son to do what he needed to do, but I had to go just as urgently, and, well, one full moon per sky per night is enough. So we kept driving.

And driving. Every time we ran over a pebble or a squirrel or a seam in the road my son yelped in discomfort and my daughter talked about flowing rivers and the sssssssssteamy sssssssssssssshower she wanted to take when we got to the hotel.

There were a decent number of cars on the road, and the road we were on was a four lane road with a 60 mph speed limit. I could see houses. I could see manufacturing plants. "Don't all these people need to gas up their cars?" I asked my captive audience. "Don't they need to go grocery shopping? Don't they need the occasional hamburger? Why is there nowhere to stop? This has GOT to be the main drag." I considered reaching underneath my seatbelt to unbuckle my pants just to relieve a little of the pressure. The only thing that stopped me was my fear that my ever swelling bladder would prevent reclosure. We went through McIntyre, Georgia, motto: "We're the home of Honey Boo Boo!" or "Plenty of perfectly nice people who aren't Honey Boo Boo or her relatives live here!" depending upon to whom the motto is being said. There was no sign, but I'm full of culturally literate factoids like that one. I thought about knocking on Ms. Boo Boo's door, but then decided I'd rather wet my pants.

I downloaded an app on my phone once upon a time called "Sit or Squat," which is brilliant. It is put out by the Charmin people. It is like a Trip Advisor or Yelp site for public bathrooms. It tells you where the potties are and whether you can sit comfortably without fear of questionable cooties or have to squat, hovering above teeming hordes of horribleness.

After some barking of instructions from the driver's seat to my smart-phone illiterate husband, and finally getting him to flip it to my 13 year old son who came out of the womb understanding All Things Electronic, we cranked up the Sit or Squat app, connected it into the phone satellites that know where I am at all times, not that this gives me the least bit of concern, and waited for it to give us a green – or red, at this point we didn't care – roll of toilet paper to indicate there was a throne in the area. No such thing popped up.

Eventually, after an hour of increasing discomfort, we realized that the closest bathroom was going to be at our hotel. I screeched into the hotel parking lot, and booked it to the lobby facilities before checking in. You should be glad to know that despite Dublin, Georgia's proximity to East Bumblefudge, there were several impressive Oscar-like statues lining the shelf above the check-in desk. My daughter asked what they were. "We're the highest rated LaQuinta in the world, and have been for five years running," the desk clerk said with obvious pride. I can't say I am a hotel expert of any kind, but I can tell you that the hotel was so much nicer than the Crack Smoking Hotel of Choice that I once stayed in to chaperone a Middle School Band Festival, that I hesitate to even use the same noun to describe them. I can also say that the bathrooms were scrupulously clean and provided a near-divine sense of relief. I'll be sure to rate them on Sit or Squat so everyone else knows it as well.

GPS Fails

I have a pretty good sense of direction, so I've never really had a problem getting from Point A to an unfamiliar Point B. Even before the days of GPS and Google Maps. Of course, I only vaguely remember those days. I rely heavily on my GPS and even when I know better I get nervous disobeying what it tells me to do. I feel like I've misbehaved when the lady who lives in the GPS in my car admonishes me to "Make a U-Turn when possible."

Recently, my husband and I went to a Boys & Girls Club fundraising event, located at the beautiful Fair Weather Farms in Monroe, GA, a place I'd never been before that night. I knew vaguely where it was, and I had the address, and so I needed nothing else. So I thought.

My car is getting on about five years old, and the information in the GPS is that old, because I am too, um, thrifty to buy the update for it. I entered the address, and looked at the turns it wanted us to make. It all made sense to me, and jived with my general sense of where the place was. We set off into the sunset. Everything was going according to plan. We weren't even really late.

That is, until we got to the new reservoir project that was in between where we were and where we wanted to be. There were detour signs, and signs that said, "No Through Traffic," but there were cars (i.e. an ambulance and a minivan full of kids) headed back in our direction on the other side of the signs, so we figured it was probably passable and there were legitimate things on the other side. We slowly slowly crossed the partially constructed dam that seemed to be made out of a giant pile of mud. We got back on a paved road, and then the GPS told us to turn right. There was a road there, maybe more of a passageway, or possibly a driveway, but whatever it was it had tire tracks visible. There was an open gate at the front of it. We stopped near the entrance, and I tried to call my friend Lindsay who was already there to see if we should chance it or if there was a better way around. Zero service. No bars at all for the phone, and no 4g or 3g or stray wi-fi to glom onto. Deprived of other options, Mike and I decided to forge forwards.

There wasn't much visibility due to the hills and valleys. The horizon was never more than 100 yards or so in front of us. We had no idea what we were driving into, although there were definitely not-yet-filled reservoir basins on either side of the ever narrowing strip of dirt road we were on. We found ourselves on a down slope. Due to the curves of the road, we couldn't get a good look at the low point. It looked kind of shiny in the waning sunlight. I couldn't tell if it was a giant puddle or a mirage.

It was in fact a giant puddle. We stopped about 20 yards away from it and contemplated what to do. According to the GPS, our destination was only a quarter mile ahead. We looked at the map and decided that even though it was a much longer way, there were enough roads to go around.

Mike was driving. He tried to back up to do a three point turn. I am six inches shorter than he is, and from my vantage point, I couldn't really tell where the edge of the road was. I hoped he could see it. At first, it didn't matter whether or not he could see it. In our minute's hesitation, the car sank into the mud and we were stuck. The tires spun. Mud kicked up in a spray. I thought about getting out and pushing, or at least relieving the car of my not inconsiderable bulk, but I was wearing impractical party clothes, and not interested in ruining my favorite boots.

Finally, we lurched backwards. I had visions of us careening over the side of the mudcliff into the unfilled reservoir basin. I checked my phone. Still no bars. Still no Wi-Fi or internet service of any kind. If we fell, I would have no way to contact anyone, and it could be days before any other moron tried to pass this road. I didn't want to die in a mudpit. When I die, I at least want to be clean. I don't want anyone, upon discovering my lifeless body, to feel compelled to say, "What in the…?"

Mike switched into drive, and we spun and then went forward a foot or so. After a seventy-five point turn, we were able to get around and start climbing back to the 'real' road. Even as we participated in one of the most epic GPS fails in recorded history, the recorded voice told us to make a U-Turn. I turned that witch off without waiting for her useless self to "recalculate."

We drove for a little while longer, and eventually came upon a road going in the direction we wanted to go in. A truck was coming back the other way. We stopped to ask the truck driver directions. He looked over his cotton sleeved arm, out of the window of his big, American pickup truck, at us in our fancy clothes in our muddy, foreign, family sedan. He told us with more kindness and patience than we deserved that we were going completely in the wrong direction, and told us to follow him. We did, and found our destination on a perfectly paved road.

I don't know who you are, Mr. Truck Driver, but you saved my life that night. I'd swap you and your practical ability to know where you are for my GPS any day. Barring that, maybe this year I should pay for the updates.

Traveling Undercaffeinated

My children, who are both naturally smart and talented at everything they attempt, not to mention extremely good looking and kind to animals, were both on teams that qualified for the National Archery in the Schools Program (NASP) national tournament in Louisville, KY in 2015. Since no one called me to ask about convenient times for this tournament, it presented a dilly of a pickle. My daughter's team was shooting Thursday afternoon. My son's team was shooting on Saturday. On Thursday I had a work obligation I couldn't get out of and my son had his final band concert and awards ceremony. So we divided and did our best to attempt to conquer.

The following plan was hatched: my daughter (Marin) and husband (Mike) would drive to Kentucky on Wednesday. Jacob and I would go to school and work, respectively, then the band concert, and fly out to meet them Friday morning. Then we'd all drive home together. Sounds like a fabulous plan, right?

The only flight I could find that cost less than renting a car (which was in and of itself exorbitant: I'm fairly certain that had we taped ourselves shut in cardboard boxes with some beef jerky and Benadryl and UPS-ed ourselves to Louisville it would have been considerably cheaper and possibly faster) left Atlanta at 7 in the morning. 7 in the morning is a reasonable time on a weekday to be doing something. However, to get on a flight that leaves at 7 in the morning, you have to leave your house (which is an hour away from the airport) at 4 in the morning, which means you have to get up at 3 in the morning, which is a time that is much easier stayed up until rather than be woken up at.

On the night before our flight, my son and I ventured to Taco Bell to eat dinner, because a quick review of the at home options included a can of Steak and Mushroom soup, an over-ripe banana, Apple Jacks, and some frost-encrusted chicken nuggets. While trying not to mindfully eat my Chicken Cantina Bowl of Despair, a Major Problem dawned on me. This was an archery tournament. Archery doesn't work well without the whole bow and arrow thing. As far as I know, when you are driving, you just throw the lot in the trunk and go where you are going. However, checking a zombie killing weapon like that on an airplane? When all you own is a soft case? I mean, I can't bring 4 ounces of shampoo with me. Certainly I couldn't bring a teenager with a deadly weapon. When we got home I 'replied all' to one of the coach's latest emails and explained the predicament. Luckily, there were lots of volunteers to help. Archery Moms and Coaches rock. They save me from me.

The day before we left, by the time we got home from the band concert (Jacob won the Duke Ellington jazz award, *thankyouverymuch*) and packed up our last minute items (our clothes had been sent on ahead with the car) it was close to midnight. We settled in for our nap and woke up to a series of screaming alarms what felt like 45 seconds later.

There is a surprising amount of traffic on the road at 4 in the morning.

We got to the airport, parked in long term parking and headed to the terminal on the shuttle bus. The bus stopped and we got off, because in my under caffeinated, not yet dawn state I forgot to consider whether or not it was our stop (it wasn't) and so we had to walk a good ways to get to our ticket counter. We didn't have any check in luggage, so we used the machine thingies. It figured out who we were, printed out boarding passes, and we walked the four hundred miles to security, what with there being construction inside the airport, necessitating little tags hanging from dangly looking crooked air vents saying things like, "Seriously? I know this looks like it is going to fall, but we promise you it is secured to something structural. This zip tie is not in any way securing this heavy metal beam. Look the other way. Hey! Isn't that the guy from that show over there?" [Actually, it said something like, "This device is securely fastened to a structural beam." But I'm no fool. I can read between the lines.]

The air vents may have been hanging there securely, but they surely were not blowing any air around. There were seventy zillion people in the Atlanta airport at 5:30 in the morning, each of them breathing hot breath and sweating. The air was thick with humanity and humid. I was hungry. I wanted coffee and food. My son, the original morning person, was speaking more or less non-stop, mostly about how he wanted to give up our place in line to venture over to the Starbucks visible through the fence. We could see the security screeners in the distance. It occurred to me that if the government was actually implanting chips in our brains in those machines, we wouldn't care, we'd raise our arms and put our shoeless feet on the yellow footprints, just for the chance to get out of that line before we smothered in the cocktail of other people's morning breath and body heat.

We finally got to the front. The TSA guy, who would probably have been too chipper for me if it were 2 in the afternoon, greeted us. What is this smiling thing he is doing? He honestly seems like he's interested in the answer when he asks us who we are. "What's your name?" he asks my son. "Jacob," says Jacob. "It's not Lori?" "No," says I. "I'm Lori." "Where's Jacob's boarding pass, then?"

I looked at the passes. Both of them said Lori. One was for me, one was for my connecting flight. Jacob's were....still in the machine, I supposed. I just grabbed two, since there were two people, and skittered off, apparently not stopping to wonder if anything else needed to be done.

To recap: it was fiveish in the morning, and my son and I were at the front of a seven mile long line of folks waiting to get through security at the Atlanta Airport. We had just been told that we only had two out of the four boarding passes we needed, and both of the ones we had read "Lori," a name my tall post-pubescent son couldn't believably claim, even with fake ID, not that he has any. It took me about 8 milliseconds to realize that in my undercaffeinated state I had left the remaining two boarding passes in the little kiosk automated machine located, in terms of how long it would take us to walk there, somewhere in Eastern Europe, from where we stood.

We started walking, and fast. Between puffs of breath, I said to my son, "See? This is why we get places early. Because we are Duffs and we have to allow for something to go completely wrong."

I went back to the kiosk, and of course in the intervening 45 minutes or so our boarding passes were no longer in the kiosk. I looked around for someone in a uniform, and finally found an official looking woman, complete with neckerchief and clipboard. You always know who is in charge in an airport because they are wearing a neckerchief.

"Apparently," I said, "The machine thingie printed out four boarding passes and we only grabbed two."

She eyed me up and down as if she were inspecting horseflesh. Squinting her eyes like she was trying to remember something, she said, "What's your last name?"

"Duff," I said.

"Ah hah." She walked over to a shelf near the ticket agents and handed me the boarding passes. I grabbed them out of her hand and pushed Jacob forward back on the hike towards security. I walked backwards some, then twisted my head in an effort to look like I was grateful for our savior's lecture on patience and responsibility.

We made it through security much more quickly this time, and got the same security agent, who I greeted by saying, "We're back! And this time he's Jacob!"

Surprisingly, we were not strip searched.

We could smell the coffee from the nearby Starbucks. I love coffee under the best and worst of circumstances, and all circumstances in between. At this point, about 5:30 in the morning, when I'd already been up long enough to watch an entire Harry Potter movie, including credits and outtakes, when I'd jogged several miles in sandals with a blue sparkly carry-on bouncing against my hip, it was a siren's song of temptation. But I forewent. We were not yet at the gate, and there was still plenty of occasion for things to go wrong.

We put our shoes back on, my son learning why wearing high top Converse sneakers to an airport was not the wisest choice in footwear, and got on the escalator to the tram. The tram stopped, and we got on. The cheerful recorded voice said, “Stop! Do not enter! The doors are about to close!” and I wondered who got paid to record that message, and how many people she beat out in the auditions. Then I wondered who does the voice on my GPS, and whether or not her husband has that kind of GPS, and passive-aggressively (or maybe all the way aggressively) refused to turn left when she said to turn left, just because it was her voice giving instruction.

I needed coffee and fast.

We got off the tram, and on the escalator so long it seemed to disappear in the clouds. As it turned out, we were in fact delivered to heaven at the top, in the form of an Einstein’s Bagels shop. There was a sign, a glorious sign, advertising a lox special (it was called salmon, but I knew better, you can’t fool this Long Island Jew, even if she does live in the deep south) and I knew what I was getting. There are very few meals I love more than a hot cup of coffee, a garlic bagel, cream cheese, a slice of onion, a juicy slice of tomato, and piles of soft orange lox. Nom nom nom. We ordered, and got our bagels to go.

By the time we got to the gate, they were already boarding the plane, so we waited until we were in our seats with our seat belts buckled (an aside: why do they demonstrate how to do a seat belt buckle? Do we really want to protect the people who can’t figure this out? Or do we have some societal obligation to save them from themselves?) and after we had greeted the poor schmo who was assigned to sit with us before digging into our breakfasts.

My stomach was audible as I unwrapped my well-deserved reward for a stressful and long morning. I unwrapped the gorgeous bagel and, in the recycled cabin air, the sharp smells of garlic and onion and fish bloomed like a mushroom cloud over my seat. I quickly wrapped it up and stuffed it in the bag, wishing I could stuff the smells in the bag along with it. I was still hungry, though, so I stuck my face in the bag and slurped up bites surreptitiously like I was sipping gin on an elementary school playground.

I ate my bagel, however ungracefully. And I drank my coffee in greedy gulps. It was all good. And we made it to Kentucky without the person next to us asking to change seats. That was good, too.

People of Hartsfield

I went to visit my parents in Ft. Myers, Florida, largely because I found an unbelievably cheap round trip flight. Of course, the "Student Driver" sticker on the plane explained the price just a little bit, as did the $50 million per carry-on bag fee.

In order to get this fare, I had to take the 7:10 a.m. flight. Rule follower that I am, I wanted to get to the airport the recommended two hours before flight time. This meant I had to be there at 5:10, which meant I had to leave the house around 4:15, which meant I had to set my alarm for somewhere around 3:30, which is more 'last night' than 'this morning.'

Every time I leave the house at 4 a.m., which is thankfully not often, I am always surprised that I'm not the only car on the road. Where are all those people going at such a ridiculous time? Due to the distinct lack of 24 hour establishments in my neighborhood, they can't be running errands, unless "Pick up pecan waffles at Waffle House" can be counted as an errand. Shift workers usually start an early shift at 7 a.m. I'd think about it some more, but I need some high test coffee in a 55 gallon drum.

I parked in the Park 'n' Drive lot (the 'a' and 'd' are removed for your convenience) and got on the shuttle bus to take me to the airport proper. Atlanta Hartsfield-(Latoya) Jackson Airport is one of the busiest airports in the world, mainly due to the fact that it is the only substantial airport in the entire state of Georgia, which is itself the largest state East of the Mississippi. Every other major city has at least two major feeder airports (Washington DC has Dulles and Reagan; Chicago has Midway and O'Hare; New York has JFK, LaGuardia, AND Newark; etc.) but not Atlanta. The result is a sprawling complex, relatively new and comfortable, with restaurants and shopping and escalators that go up so high they vanish into the distance.

At 5 o'clock in the morning on the shuttle bus, there were a few collegiate looking people, a few business looking people, me, and a family of four with two young children. The family of four did 100% of the talking on the shuttle bus, including but not limited to a 10 minute conversation about whether or not a two year old boy was going to finish eating his "nana." (As I type this, I realize it looks like the kid was being encouraged to eat his grandmother: I promise you it looked like a standard issue banana.)

Once at the airport, while standing on line for the kiosk, I looked at my phone for the first time in the morning, and saw an email letting me know that my flight had a four hour delay, but I should get to the airport at the regular time anyway. I looked up at the departures board, and it said my flight was on time. I didn't know who to believe.

It was a relatively uneventful trip through security, the highlight of which was a disgruntled TSA worker, clearly tired of the sheep-like nature of the people on the lines she was herding, who loudly tried to convince people that there was a better way. "I promise you there are two lines here. Some of you really can go to the left. That's right, go around all these people who won't get off the line on the right. Two lines here, then it splits into four around that post. I promise you that's really a line." "Baaaa," said the sheeple, as they stayed on the right line. No government yahoo was going to tell THEM what to do.

Turned out the flight really was delayed four hours. There were a LOT of irate and sleepy people at the gate. For purposes of solidarity, I pretended to be irritated, too. But between you and me, I was secretly pleased. I was given a $7 food voucher. (At airport prices, this buys you a fun sized Snickers bar.) I was given a place to sit and no one to talk to, or, more to the point, no one to talk to me, and the ability to crawl inside my head and clear out some cobwebs. There was email to return, a million books on my Kindle, several articles already written in my head that needed transcribing, and some seriously high quality people watching.

There is no better place on Earth to people watch than a major airport. I played "where you do think they are going and why" with the voices in my head. I questioned some fashion choices, including why any woman would wear heels in order to walk down a hallway longer than most streets in metropolitan areas. I wondered if I was the only one who thought of Ferdinand the Bull every time she saw someone with a ring in the septum of his nose. I wondered how certain people got their hair to stay that way, and whether they did that on purpose. I smiled at little children and babies, and sympathized with their parents, who were schlepping car seats and trying to figure out how to use the restroom without any tiny little fingers touching anything irredeemably disgusting. (Been there, sister.) In the restroom, watching a line of women scrubbing their hands like surgeons, I wondered what their hygiene routines were like when no one was looking. It's fun watching old men try to figure out how to use their smart phones to entertain themselves when they finish the paper. I also found the time to bemoan my ridiculously short shins that require me to lift my heels in order to get my lap flat enough to balance a laptop on.

I am sad that I have four fewer hours with which to spend with my parents. I love them dearly and I know that, at the ripe old age of 45, that I am in the lucky minority to have both of them not only alive but married to each other. But if I had to lose four hours, this wasn't the worst way to do it.

Um…I Forgot

I tried to slip one of my daughter's teachers a twenty dollar bill the other day, but she wouldn't take it. I think she just felt hinky taking unexpected cash money from me, though my guess is if I had handed her a $20 gift card to an office supply store she'd have taken it. I get emails all the time asking for paper towels and tissues and hand sanitizer and plastic spoons and blue food coloring and pipe cleaners and glue sticks and sugar cubes. Only rarely do I manage to actually get these things to the school. I feel badly about my failure, because I know if the parents don't come through the teachers have to reach into their own pockets, or the parents who are more coordinated than I am end up taking the lion's share of the burden.

There is so much remembering and coordinating involved. I have to note what I'm supposed to get, buy it, give it to my daughter, and make sure she gets it to school, assuming it isn't something too unwieldy or messy for her to bring on her own. That's like four remembers for one simple task. I'm lucky to get one remember in before I forget.

As I type this, it is the third day of the third quarter of school. My son, who is in seventh grade, and so you'd think he'd be too old for that sort of thing, has already had requests for gummy bears, red Twizzlers, toothpicks, and Play Doh, in addition to the standard compliment of paper towels and tissues. I wrote these things on a piece of paper as I left work the other day, knowing I was running by the grocery store to pick up a few things anyway. I made up a New Year's resolution on the spot. This year, 2015, I was going to be the kind of Mom that came through for the teachers; the kind of Mom who made sure her kids had what they needed to make edible strands of DNA and learn geometry through clay.

I remembered to buy exactly none of these things. I didn't even remember that I was supposed to buy these things until the next day when I put my hand in my coat pocket and found the list I'd so carefully written.

Generally speaking, I'm a pretty responsible person. I show up where I'm supposed to show up when I'm supposed to show up there. I get my paperwork in on time. I get holiday cards out before the actual holiday (ok, except for this year) and pay all my bills in a timely fashion. I've never run out of gas in my car. There are always clean clothes in my closet, and in my children's closet. Although there may not be any food I *want* to eat in my house, there is generally food I *can* eat in my house, and some of it even has nutritional value.

So why can't I remember these things? Isn't my children's education a priority? Thinking back, I can't remember my teachers ever asking my parents for things like this. I don't ever remember dragging shopping bags full of supplies on the school bus. Of course, I can't remember any hands-on type projects beyond fourth grade, either. Maybe this is the price we pay for more creative teaching methods. I guess it is just hard for my brain to latch on to the fact that a 79 cent box of toothpicks is related to my son's education in any significant way.

Of course, it isn't like I'm the kind of person who remembers these kinds of things in any context. When I'm supposed to bring something from home into work, my friends will leave Post-It notes on the steering wheel of my car and text me at least twice during the night and once in the morning.

I am proud to say that I have never missed a Court date in twenty years of practicing law, although about a half dozen times I have driven to the wrong Courthouse.

So what's the difference? Why am I completely reliable in one context, and completely unreliable in another?

I think I knew once, but I forgot.

A Tale of Two Chins

I'm old, but not so old that I am completely afraid of technology. I embrace it, for the most part, for all the things it can do for us, and the ways it can make things easier. One of the best things it can do for me is allow me to keep my big fat butt in my chair. I mean, it allows me to save gas and therefore money and the environment. It has nothing to do with how lazy I am. Nothing at all.

I'm not just talking about online shopping, my preferred retail method. I've edited documents in real time with people in France via Google Hangout. I regularly meet with Suzen from Omaginarium via Skype. We've never met in person, but we've met a lot, and I consider her a friend. I've called into group meetings before via telephone, but that's usually a slog. You can't tell who is talking, and it is easy to zone out and lose track of what is going on with no visual stimulus save Candy Crush on your cell phone. I don't like phoning in meetings.

Recently, I 'attended' a meeting via an online meeting service. There wasn't much technical prowess required to attend this meeting, which is why I was able to attend it. I clicked a link on an email and typed in my name. Then my face popped up on a screen along with everyone else's. My face. My tired, day worn face. (It was a four o'clock meeting.) I tried to make myself go away, but the best I could figure out what to do was make my face small. No matter what I did it looked like I was being reflected in a fun house mirror.

I couldn't get the angle right. The only way I could prop my laptop on my desk so the webcam could see me was at an angle that highlighted the multitude of chins underneath my jawline. My slack face, my resting face, looks angry at best, but if I smiled, I looked like a grinning idiot smiling for no reason than the sheer joy of sitting through a two hour meeting. But if I didn't, my mouth formed an upside down semicircle, kind of like Beaker's from the Muppets. (I prefer to think of it as rainbow shaped rather than frowny shaped.) My eyes are small under the best of circumstances. Looking down towards the screen of my laptop, they look closed, as if I were sleeping. If I deliberately opened them, I look liked Jack Nicholson in the Shining.

To top it off, I thought this was a call-in meeting when I sat down. So I had already changed into my gym clothes. Everyone else was still dressed like a responsible grownup with ties and suit jackets and whatnot. I was wearing a Chik-Fil-A Bowl T-Shirt from 2013. I thought about changing back, but then everyone would have seen me.

Sometimes I took a swig from my water bottle. If I saw the action echoed on the screen, I cringed with my lack of grace. In my twisted brain, I saw a dopey St. Bernard lapping up water and then slobbering all over the sofa. My nose itched, and I was afraid to scratch it for fear someone would misinterpret the gesture.

I wasn't sure where to look. My instinct was to look at the person who was talking, even though they couldn't tell that I was trying to make virtual eye contact. Some people didn't have webcams, so you couldn't see them, only hear them and a little bubble would pop up to tell you who was talking. When they were talking, it seemed rude to stare at the screen, which meant directly looking at other people who are also listening to the speaker. I wouldn't do that in real life, but what else was I supposed to do? If I looked at something else in my office then my face went drifting off on the screen and everyone could see it. So, if I looked at anyone else I felt like a stalker. If I looked at my own face, well, yuck.

This was a complete distraction. This is a very serious meeting that I am attending, and this was a very functional, efficient, cost-effective, and time saving way to attend it. It is my own problem that I was having trouble focusing on the content, because every time I glanced at myself inadvertently during a discussion I thought "woof" instead of, "how does this compare to fiscal year 2014?" which would have been a more on-topic thought to have had.

This was a group of relatively high powered people with impressive titles at the top of their professions. We were in this meeting because of our supposed ability to make intellectual contributions. No one gave a rat's patootie if my mascara was sliding down my cheek or if the shape of my eyebrows was more 'caterpillar' than 'arched' as it was more than three weeks after the latest waxing. Odds are, no one but me noticed that I was wearing a t-shirt, since you could only see the top of my shoulders. Odds are, if they were concerned with anything, it was their own web-cam distorted faces on display. I was not asked to be a part of this meeting because of my good looks or ability to dress myself. So why was I obsessed with this? Why was I more worried about looking unattractive than saying something stupid? I wasn't at all worried about what I had to say. If I had attended the meeting in person, I would have been completely unaware of my physical self and, while my mind might have wandered during the more boring bits, I wouldn't have been obsessing about my looks. Then again, in person I don't have to look at me the whole time, either.

I could guess a thousand reasons why this is, none of which matter, because the bottom line is that I am well aware that my priorities are absolutely out of whack. In this context, what's on the inside is the only thing that matters. And what's on the outside isn't half as bad as the insecure eleven year old stuck inside me thinks. So why can't I make her go back to middle school where she belongs when I go out and play with the grownups?

You figure it out, you let me know.

Critters

Critters

Roadkill Cupcakes

My second book, which if you haven't read yet you should and I will pause right now while you go order three copies (one for you, and two for gifts) is called "The Armadillo, the Pickaxe, and the Laundry Basket." In order to celebrate the release, I had a party and invited everyone on the internet and their plus-ones.

The theme of the party was, naturally, Armadillos and Laundry Baskets. I left the pickaxes out of my decorating schemes since I wanted people to come close, not to worry that there was a serial killer in the room. I filled a laundry basket with towels, a bottle of Tide, and many many copies of the book. My daughter made me the following promotional picture, which I posted everywhere because I thought it was funny.

photo credit Marin Duff

Marin, who at the time was eleven years old and in 6th grade, and therefore an expert in all things humiliating, was horrified. She thought she'd made the picture as a joke. "Mom!" She said. "I can't believe you posted that picture in public! That's the kind of thing that OTHER people post to make fun of you."

Maybe for most people. But me? I have zero shame, and get my greatest belly laughs laughing at myself. Why should I deprive others of the privilege? In fact, when one of my good friends saw the galley for "The Armadillo, the Pickaxe, and the Laundry Basket," she saw some of the pictures of me in there and said, "It's a good thing you don't care what people think of you."

I tried to find cupcake toppers with armadillos on them, or some kind of armadillo shaped candy, but came up short unless I wanted to spend $11.00 PER CUPCAKE TOPPER. Excuse me. No. For $11.00 I can get two whole pizzas at Little Caesar's. Including tax. I eventually landed on getting custom made buttons for twenty cents each which I placed on top of store bought cupcakes. Of course, on my computer screen the image filled the screen. I found a great armadillo picture and put the title of the book in an obnoxious colored font so it would stand out. I knew in theory that the diameter was one inch, but, well, I've never been a good independent judge of measurement. The tiny little buttons looked like weird brown smudges with some kind of neon green cuneiform print. Many of my middle aged friends brought out the reading glasses and still couldn't read it.

I wanted cupcakes that were obviously armadillo themed. So, I went to that friend I love to hate, Pinterest. I found these:

Cute, right? And seemingly easy. Regular cupcakes with broken up Nutter Butters and cut up circus peanuts. (An aside, who actually buys circus peanuts because they like to eat them? Blech.) While buying the supplies, I found that Publix was out of circus peanuts (Seriously? Who bought the entire stock?) so I bought orange candy slices and Bugles as a substitute. I told my kids we were going to have fun watching me try to be a "Pinterest Mom."

I have to say that my armadillo looked more realistic than the Pinterest cupcakes, in that most of the armadillos I've seen in person are some variation of roadkill. Our Nutter Butters wouldn't stand up straight. Our black-dot-eyes looked like hollow, haunted, empty sockets. The shiny sides of the cut up orange slices looked vaguely like exposed brain matter, and the Bugles like exposed bone. (But be honest here: how many of you, at least once in your life, have put Bugles over the tips of your fingers in order to make your hands look like witches' hands?)

Our cupcakes looked like this:

We only made those four, and then we gave up, resigning ourselves to the fact that we were not a successful Pinterest family and would just have to eat all the Nutter Butters sans cupcake.

Still, the party was fun, even if a few people accidentally pierced their tongues trying to lick the frosting off the armadillo buttons I stuck on the top of the non-roadkill cupcakes. I guess the moral of this story is therefore two-fold: a) know your artistic limitations; and b) don't lick anything with a pin on the back.

Armadillo Redux

My house has a history with armadillos. In fact, as I may have mentioned, but it bears repeating, the name of my second book is "The Armadillo, The Pickaxe, and the Laundry Basket," based on the time when an armadillo tunneled its way into my bedroom one night. The armadillo and his army of armadillo buddies had torn down all the duct work in the crawl space in my house and used the resultant hole to climb in by bedroom to do whatever it is that armadillos do when they find themselves on Berber carpet.

So you will forgive us if we don't particularly care for armadillos in our yard. I know they are here because, well, if looks are any indication, they are dinosaur remnants and have been here for thousands of years, if not millions, and that technically I put *my* house on *their* land, but, well, I'd like to think there are some privileges that come with being the dominant predator on the planet and the top of each and every food chain.

I'm not a vegetarian. Anyone who remembers so fondly the foodgasm she had while eating a rack of lamb at The Georgia Pine can't exactly complain about killing animals. Still, I believe we shouldn't just kill for goofers, and if you're going to kill it you should at least try to eat it. I think about that from time to time when I flick a Daddy Long Legs into oblivion just because it is tickling my arm. What right do I have to kill another being just because it irritates me? Well, it isn't like I can look a horsefly in its eye(s) and explain to it that I will live and let live if it just quits buzzing by my ear and promises not to bite. Insects don't bargain or understand. I mean, we're all God's critters and whatnot, but I'll bet even God smacks a mosquito if it lands on His Holy Face.

But back to the armadillos. Lately, we've been finding a suspicious number of armadillo-sized tunnels in our yard near our house. Given what it cost us to replace the duct work last year, and given the proximity of the holes to the in-ground posts and poles that prevent our house from sinking into the ground and/or falling over, those holes are no bueno. Likewise, the buggers that dig them are even less bueno.

Last night, my husband and I were rocking and swinging in our respective seats on our porch, ducking when the bats that live behind our shutters flew out to eat bugs, and listening to the night birds and making small talk. My husband doesn't hear very well, which probably explains the volume of his speaking voice, and the fact that he is surprised that his humming to himself drowns out any other noise in the house. I, however, can hear perfectly well. Therefore, I heard a skritch-skritch-scritch and the sound of dirt landing on leaves, and he did not. I said, as much to myself as anyone else, "That sounds like an armadillo."

Mike, who had been lulled half asleep by the rhythm of the glider he was sitting in, sprang up, instantly awake and alert, like the fireman he used to be. He ran down the stairs and saw the armadillo. In a matter of only seconds, he rapidly shifted from mild mannered retired guy to emergency first responder to Carl the Groundskeeper from Caddyshack.

He was going to get that armadillo.

Generally when he wants varmints to remove themselves from our yard, he gets a low powered pellet gun and shoots tiny plastic pellets at them. I'm not even sure this 'weapon' would put your eye out at point blank range, not that we're going to test this theory. If that doesn't work, he might ramp it up to metal bb's. But not this time. Nope. This was no catch and release situation. He got his .25 pistol, his "Baby Baretta," the gun he says he'd like to have with him if he's ever in a knife fight, and quickly discovered that he didn't actually have any ammunition for it. After a ridiculously lengthy search for bullets in all the places bullets might be in our house, he gave up.

Not the armadillo, though. He was still digging, oblivious to the efforts made to send him to armadillo heaven.

Eventually, Mike unearthed his 22 caliber bolt-action rifle and was able to locate ammunition for it. By this time it was close to midnight, but this didn't prevent him from going out in the yard and shooting. This was at our lake house located in the muddy armpit of Lake Oconee, right across the lake from the Oconee National Forest, which is further out in the middle of nowhere than our regular house, and located in a place which has no laws I'm aware of that would prevent you from firing a rifle in your yard at midnight. Especially during deer and duck season, you hear a lot of rifle reports, all during the day and night.

Despite the fact that my husband has all kinds of advanced firearm training, and can aim at things and actually hit them most of the time, it took five blasts to finish off the armored armadillo, which skittered into the crawl space under our house to die in peace.

I've never shot and killed anything in my life. This is partly because I grew up on Long Island where the population density is such that if you fire a gun in any direction at any time of day or night you are guaranteed to hit another person so no one except bad guys shoot them at all. It is also partly because my aim is so poor that even if I wanted to shoot and kill something, odds are good I would only maim something unintentional, probably myself.

I started my legal career as a prosecutor and, for professional reasons, had to handle a lot of guns. I decided that it would probably a good idea for me to learn about them. My husband Mike, who was at the time pre-retired and therefore a working police officer, took me in the woods behind our house, setting up milk jugs filled with water as targets. He gave me his .25 baby Beretta and a short tutorial on how it worked. It was a tiny thing, almost cute, smaller than the palm of my hand.

Confident that I could perform a simple task like pulling a trigger while holding the gun in a steady direction, I took aim at my milk jug victim and squeezed the trigger. The force of the recoil from such a tiny little device startled me, and without thinking, I threw my arm backwards and upwards. Mike caught my arm and gently removed the gun from my hand. "You get one bullet at a time," he said, removing the clip.

I shot a few more times that afternoon, but that was the last day I pulled the trigger on anything. I haven't even played paintball. The world is a much better place if people other than me have access to firearms.

So needless to say, when an armadillo needed killing in our yard, it was not me who was going to do it. My husband, the ex-police sergeant with a sniper-like ability to hit the things he aims at (he claims to be able to hit carpenter bees with a bb gun, which explains the little metal pellets all over my deck) dispatched the creature with only five rifle slugs (his excuse: it was dark, and the armadillo was small and skittery and armor plated), and as a result, I now had a dead armadillo in the crawl space.

Under the best of circumstances, armadillos smell. Under the worst, they stink to high heaven (and low heaven, and every heaven in between) and carry leprosy.

The next morning, I went to plant some moonflowers in the flower bed next to our deck. I sank down to my knees to dig the hole and saw, with metaphorical x's over his eyes, a remarkably intact armadillo through the lattice separating the flowerbed from the crawl space. I don't know how I didn't smell it before I saw it.

This is Georgia. This is summer. Dead things get rank quickly.

It was time to force the Great Armadillo Hunter to do something about his prey.

It was no small task getting the armadillo out. It took thick leather gloves, a shovel, and a rope. Mike tied a rope around its tail and somehow dragged it out. He then stood up, with a stinky possum on the half-shell dangling by his side.

I wanted to feel badly for my part in killing an animal I had no intentions of eating.

But I couldn't. It looked pre-historic. It looked mean. It smelled worse than my 13 year old son's running shoes. It had nasty looking prickly hairs sticking out from the bottom. Its only purpose in the biosphere that I could tell was to dig up the foundation of my house and spread disease.

We thought briefly about tying it to a tree in the yard of the neighbors whose dogs are always getting out and pooping in our yard, but we're better people than that. Not better enough to refrain from the fantasy, but better enough not to actually do it. We thought about throwing it in the lake and letting it be fish food. Instead, we gave it a semi-proper burial in an unmarked grave in the woods.

Thank God Mike was there to deal with it. If it were up to me, I probably would have just let it tear down our house, one clawful of dirt at a time.

Bats vs. Snakes

There has been a family of bats residing behind the shutters on the porch of my house on Lake Oconee for more than a year now. They don't really bother me much. I like that they eat bugs. I like that they don't bother anyone during the day, and during the night they look awfully cool silhouetted by the moonlight. I don't particularly care for the pile of pebbly bat guano that builds up underneath the shutter, though. We sweep it into an old bucket because it is fabulous fertilizer. In fact, without looking it up, I happen to know off the top of my head that it can be a lucrative cash crop: it is the primary export of the Island Nation of Nauru, for example. There is a very live and let live attitude between the Duff family and the bats. Marginally symbiotic, neither party has any interest in disrupting the relationship.

One Monday morning, not long after the Great Armadillo Infestation described in the previous chapter, I left my family sprawled out in their respective beds and trucked it into town to Take Care of Business. The day rocked along without incident, until early afternoon, when my children started sending me the "I'm boooooooooooooooooored" texts, because those poor deprived children were being forced to spend the afternoon with their father in an environment with a lake to swim in and a yard to play in but (brace yourself) no Wi-Fi. They were begging me to come get them and take them home because they just couldn't take it anymore.

Naturally, I had very little sympathy.

Then, at 4:41, I received the following text from my son: "Pllleeeeaaaasssseeee there's a freaking king snake in the shutters the bats are freaking out and all the babies are crawling all over the yard dad was saying he was going to take down the shutters to clean them out and I made a joke about that being another three year project and he got mad."

I mean, I hate missing out on a beautiful summer day on the lake with my family as a general rule, but missing a blog-worthy incident like that one? Pure tragedy.

Before I got a chance to respond, "WE SAVED LIVES" came via text from his sister.

Me: Huh????

Marin: Lives would've been lost without me and Dad

Me: ????????

Marin: A snake attacked the baby bats and we saved them.

[At this point, I pictured my daughter dressed like Xena, Warrior Princess, ululating and swinging a broadsword over her head towards the snake, which immediately dropped the baby bat in its mouth and slithered off, frightened. As an aside, how tasty could a baby bat possibly be? How many nutrients could be in that small body so full of tiny bones and flaps of skin? They're probably the chicken wings of the snake world's diet. And not even the drummette part.]

Me: How?

Marin: They crawled away from the massacre and we put them in a bucket before the snake could attack them again.

Me: My hero.

Marin: And one of them got away without our help but we found it in a wet ball of sadness. It looked like it was about to die.

Me: I'm assuming you're nursing it back to health?

Marin: Yea

Me: That's my girl.

That is, in fact, my girl. She has to pick a community service project for her upcoming bat mitzvah (seriously – no pun intended) and she has toyed with the idea of something involving "saving ugly animals, because everyone wants to save the cute, cuddly ones, and no one cares about the ugly ones."

She's right. There are no "save the blobfish" rallies or t-shirts I've ever seen. No one buys a cockroach-shaped stuffed animal, or says "awwwww!" every time they see a rat. I'm not aware of anyone else who thinks "save them" towards either side in the battle of bats vs. snakes. I think it's awesome that she immediately thinks of the underdog animals, the ones that might be misunderstood simply because they aren't cute. I hope she feels the same about people.

In the meantime, I seriously hope she doesn't get rabies.

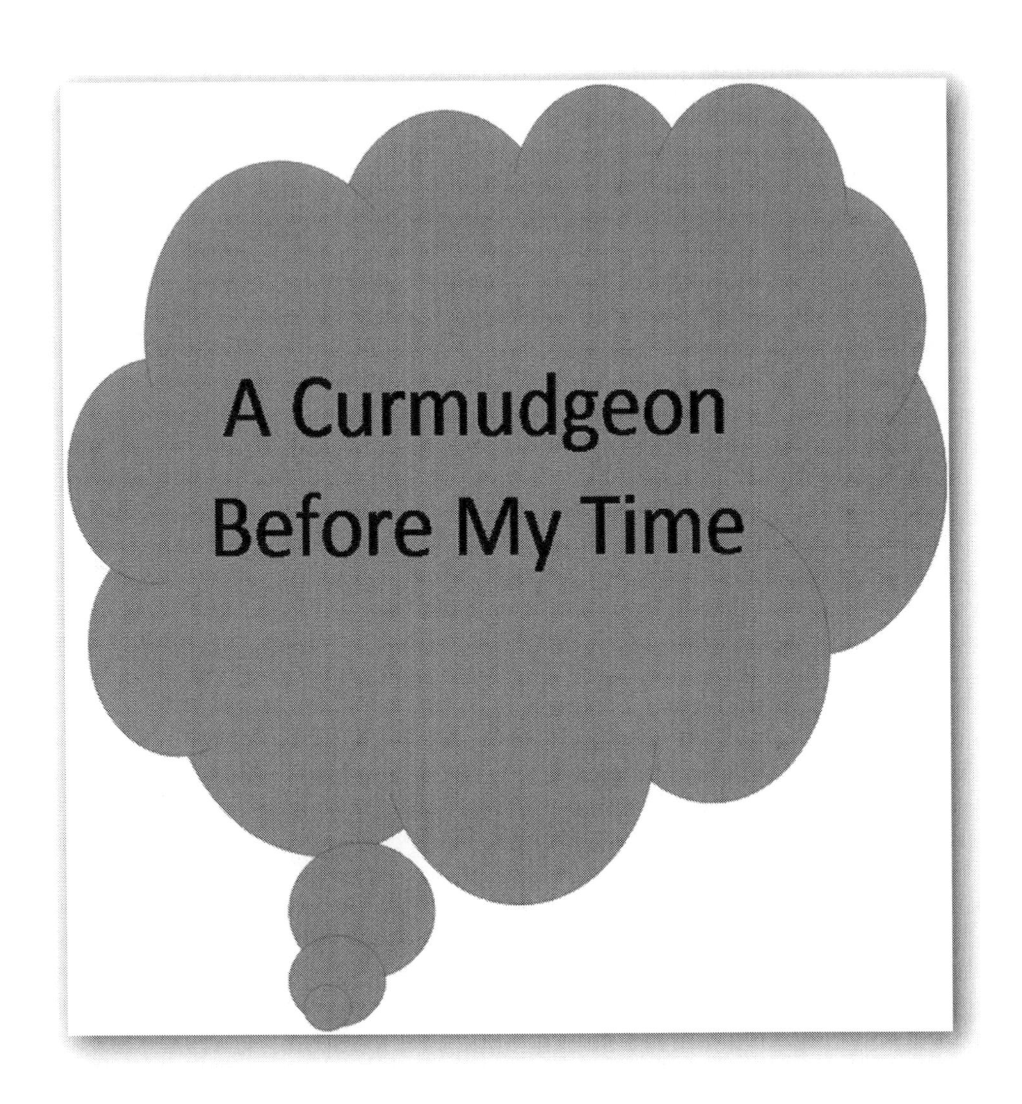
A Curmudgeon
Before My Time

A Curmudgeon Before My Time

Uncommon Courtesy

I think as a public service, I am going to use this space to review a little bit of basic math: the shortest distance between two points is a straight line.

Let me back up a minute and tell you why I am saying this. It seems to me that every single time I find myself in a parking lot of any kind, there is someone who is on-foot in front of me. Now, I totally get that there is a lot of mandatory on-foot traffic in a parking lot. You park your car, you get out of it, and then you walk towards the building, often having to cross through ways in which other cars are driving. Sometimes, like at a school, (which is where I lost my mind this morning) there are cars dropping off people who then get out of the car and walk towards the building.

There are many times when you can't park directly in front of the door, or drop someone off right in front. So I *get* that there has to be walking.

I don't get that there has to be diagonal or zig-zag walking. I don't get that you have to walk three abreast in the center of the roadway. I don't get that you, a healthy young person, have to walk so slowly that I have to look closely to see that you are moving at all. I truly-uly-uly don't get why you can't put down your iPhone for five seconds so you can cross the road while looking at the road and the other people and cars on it. Or sometimes I think people walking do the opposite and are looking through my windshield trying to find my eyes behind my sunglasses just to telepathically communicate the message, "Yeah. You can wait for ME. I. Don't. Care."

Sometimes I'll even say out loud, "Go Go Gadget Copter" and push an imaginary button on the dashboard which pops the helicopter blades out of my moon roof and gets them spinning and kicking up a dust storm before taking off into the distance that the slow walkers find themselves choking on dirt and jet fuel fumes.

So, since common courtesy has officially been renamed uncommon courtesy given its rarity, I would like here to list a few basic rules that I think will be non-controversial:

1. When walking in a roadway, walk single-file and on the side. If you must cross the road, do it at a corner, or, if no corner, in a straight line, and at the very least put some pep in your step, assuming you are physically able to do so.
2. When getting on or off an elevator, train, bus, or anything else that comes to you and has doors that open, the people getting off the elevator, etc., have the right of way. This is because they are making room for you to get on/in. And because I said so.
3. When you go through a door of any kind, look behind you. If there is someone within, say, 20 feet behind you coming towards the door, HOLD THE DOOR.
4. If you are in line at a store, and you have enough groceries to feed a 13 year old boy for 6 hours (if this doesn't sound like a mountain of food, you haven't ever tried to keep a 13 year old boy fed) and the person behind you has a simple tin of Fancy Feast, let the person behind you get ahead of you.

5. No matter how interesting your telephone conversation may be to you, or might be to the world at large if both sides of it were heard, if we are standing two feet from each other in a public place, your side of the conversation is not interesting to me, and is probably interrupting the thoughts and conversations of everyone around you. I know I feel physically assaulted.
6. If I am in my car at a red light, and my windows are up, my air conditioner is on, and my own radio is on, and yet your music is so loud that it is rattling the fillings in my molars, your radio is probably too loud.

I'm going to stop here at a cool half dozen. Though truthfully, I could probably fill a book, and might with the least bit of encouragement. Now that I think about it: this is that book. You're welcome.

Smell Pollution

I've never been a real estate agent, and I'm not a particularly good salesperson, mainly because if someone says they don't want something, or even gives the remotest signal with their body language that they don't want to talk to me or wants me to change the topic, it seems kind of rude to force them into it. That said, I'm not an idiot, and I'm pretty sure that no sales pitch ever in the history of the world contained the phrases "down wind from a paper mill" or "the nearby railway blows a warning signal every day at two a.m."

No one likes loud, unwanted noises. No one gets glad when a car drives by their house with a thumping baseline that shakes the window. No one wants to be around the guy who smells like the bait from his fishing trip or the live cultures on his sweat socks. We don't want the hotel room that looks out on the giant blinking neon sign. I'm not aware of anyone who has ever said, "Yes! The neighbor's dog won't stop barking! This is the best night of my life!" We don't want ugly cell towers in our backyards or billboards concealing the views of, well, sometimes the other billboards. We've all been choked in an elevator with someone who thinks one bottle of perfume equals one application.

The point is this: we don't like to have our senses assaulted. We don't like to have to smell stinky smells, we don't like to see ugly things, and we don't want noise pollution. There are laws against such things, and no one I know of thinks there shouldn't be. I'm going to assume that so far I haven't said a single controversial thing.

All of this occurred to me one day as I went out to eat in a restaurant which had outdoor seating. I was sitting indoors, but I had a clear view of everyone outside. Everyone seemed normal enough. Then a woman walked by and stopped to read the menu which was posted on the wall near the outdoor seating. There was nothing unusual about this woman. Average height, average size, your basic brown hair of average length, normal everyday type clothing. But she was smoking a cigarette. Great clouds of gray funk swirled around her head and tapped a few diners on the shoulder.

No one said anything to her. A few people wrinkled their noses, but from my vantage point, all I could see were people going about their collective businesses and eating their dinners.

Let me say this: I cannot bear the smell of cigarette smoke. Not only is it an unpleasant smell, but it is a migraine trigger for me, and the more I am around it, the more likely I am to get a whanging headache that only a lobotomy and/or hours spent in a dark room under the influence of prescription drugs can remedy. I have several friends who are allergic to it. No one I know likes the smell. I mean, seriously, have you ever been in a Yankee Candle store? They have candles that smell like every single thing: there are even separate candles for Clean Linen and Clean Cotton and a completely different one for Fresh Laundry. Every fruit, every herb, leathery smells, florals, beachy, pine-y, savory, sweet, and spicy. But there is not a single 'flavor' that smells anything like "Unfiltered Camels."

So I'm not going to talk about the health risks of smoking. That horse took its last, raspy, emphysemic breath a few years ago. I'm not going to beat it. Neither am I going to talk about physical addiction or any of that. I'm just going to talk about the stink. The stink that fills your nostrils and makes your risotto taste like it was prepared on the set of *Mad Men*. The stink that clings to my hair and lingers in the way I wish hair products would. The stink that says, "the person making the stink doesn't give a rat's patootie about you, your health, your senses, or your general enjoyment of life."

I don't know why we put up with this. We have noise ordinances. We have zoning laws which prohibit certain unsightly things from existing in certain places. No one would expect us to grin and bear a neighbor's loud stereo or home pork rendering business. In fact, most people I know wish there were more 'nuisance' ordinances like this because these small, grain-of-sand-in-your-sandal nuisances can really ruin your day.

Most smokers I know have the decency to be embarrassed that they can't kick the habit, and are fairly considerate about going 'somewhere else' around the corner or away from others whilst upping their nicotine to blood ratio. I appreciate those gestures. Even more, I appreciate the folks who have switched over to those electronic cigarettes. I'm not sure how they work, but somehow they deliver nicotine through an inhale/ exhale method, and the 'smoke' is actually steam that smells like exactly nothing.

Ah, yes. The sweet sweet smell of nothing at all.

I Wish I Smoked

I had reason to say this today: I wish I smoked.

I mean, I don't really wish I smoked. I cannot bear the smell of cigarette smoke, and I have no interest in a permanent hacking cough, heart disease, or lung and/or mouth cancer. I just wish I had a vice like smoking that was socially acceptable.

For example, when I have my lawyer hat on, I will often participate in mediations, either representing clients or as the mediator. At times, these mediations can get long and hairy. By hour seven everyone's nerves are frayed. Often, a party who is a smoker will say something like, "I just need to step outside and have a cigarette." They do, no one tells them they can't, and they come back looking visibly more relaxed, if perhaps a bit stinkier.

I'm jealous of them. I wish I had a reason to step out of a stressful situation for ten minutes and do whatever it was that calmed me down.

None of us in my office smoke. We do, however, keep packs of bubblegum cigarettes at the office. Whenever one of us is obviously having a difficult time on the phone, one of us will walk over and offer the frustrated individual a cigarette. She will pop it in her mouth and blow the powdered sugar out of the tip in an exaggerated way. It's a joke. It makes us laugh, it breaks the tension, it lets the other know we sympathize with her plight, but it isn't quite the same as the actual vice.

I've given a startling amount of thought to this. I'm not much of a brain-altering substance person. I don't want chemical release in any form, prescription drugs, or even alcohol in these situations. I like to be in control of my faculties in stressful situation, or at least as much control as my addled brain will let me have. I need my wits about me. I'm not giving that up to a bottle: prescription, over the counter, or long-necked.

I think what appeals to me about smoking is this: first, you get to physically remove yourself from the situation. No matter how far you are from the exit, you get to go outside and get some fresh air, and people will just wait for you. (Of course, smoking in 'fresh air' de-freshifies it as soon as the match is struck, but that's a rant you've already heard.) You get to experience a sensual pleasure that involves the regulation of your breathing.

I'm pretty sure that if I could step outside, grab on to a doorframe and stretch my spine (my favorite stretch, which I am tall enough to do in most – but not all – doorframes) and practice my deep breathing in silence I could get the same effect. Un-conditioned air, processed clean by trees and greenery, and not having been recycled through everyone else's lungs, especially when paired with sunshine or pretty stars, has the tendency to sweep the cobwebs out of my brain.

But how do I do that? How do I just stop what I'm doing and tell other people to just hold up and wait for me by saying, "I need some fresh air" and then going to hang on a doorframe or bend over in a boring blue suit and touch my toes and take deep lungfuls of air without looking or sounding like a complete idiot? Especially when odds are good that there isn't actually any fresh air because standing right next to me will be someone with a cigarette.

I propose this: during the course of any day, we all get two time outs. Time-outs are not to last more than 15 minutes each. We can use our time out cards whenever we want, and people, even people who outrank us, have to respect them. Just like in basketball, whether time out is called by the coach or a player, time out the clock stops short. When you play a time out card in real life, the clock just stops. If you won't honor someone else's time out, it is a technical foul, and you have to give up two of your own time outs. During time out, no one can question what we are doing (so long as it is legal) or make fun of us (to our faces) for whatever stupid ritual calms us down as individuals.

Go ahead. Suck your thumb. Cuddle your teddy bear. Sing "I Will Survive" at the top of your lungs. Drink your chocolate milk. Eat a Cadbury Egg. I don't care. Just come back with your head clear, and we can get things done.

I'm Too Old for Overtime

I watched the Duke Blue Devil/UNC Tar Heel college basketball game the other night. As a Duke alum, I'm pretty sure I signed something upon graduation saying that they could take away my diploma if I didn't watch this game every year. Which is fair enough, because I would never not watch it on purpose.

Due to the magic of DVRs and season passes, I don't ever watch anything when it is actually on, and I have no idea what channel most things are aired on or what number goes with what channel. I know we get ESPN, for example, but I could not tell you what channel ESPN is. My DVR knows, and that's all I need to know. I'm spoiled out of my mind, and don't ever watch commercials.

So, when my family made an emergency Wal-Mart run at 8:00 p.m. to replace a leaking coffee maker, I was unconcerned that we would be back in time for the 9 o'clock tip off. The DVR would catch it, and I could fast forward through commercials and the blahblah of half time, and watch everything in relatively real time with no problem. We got home at 9:30, I cued up the game, and settled in to watch in the rocker recliner.

Which is another 'used to' that I don't do. I used to be unable to sit during exciting ball games, much less recline leisurely. I would pace around the room, or even drop to my knees in front of the television, certain that the great waves of sincere caring would affect the trajectory of the ball. I still believe I can care enough to affect an orange piece of rubber several hundred miles away from me that got flung a half hour before I'm actually seeing it, but now I believe I can do it while sitting. I also throw my hands into the air when the mood strikes. In this way the players know I am on their side.

The La-Z-Boy, however, may be another story. I felt like I had the wrong momentum Reclined with my feet up (the only way I can exist without falling over after 10:00 p.m.) all the up and down excitement of an exciting game was first a full body 90 degree tilt instead of a mere up and down on the Y axis. It was like doing crunches. I'm supposed to be *watching* sports. Not working up a sweat.

This was quite a game. It went into overtime. Having learned the DVR lesson years ago, I always set it to record for extra time in a sporting event. You don't want to invest two emotional hours in a game to not see the last few moments which determine the winner.

Let me first say this: I am too old for overtime. It was after 11:00 p.m. on a work night and my heart was pumping. I had to get up to be at an 8:30 a.m. meeting. I was tired from the day and exhausted from the game. I get how the players manage it – they are teenagers, for the most part, and in hella good shape. The coaches? Not a clue. I guess they aren't soft and squishy and nine to fivey like us desk jockeys. I'm also guessing they can go home and sleep until late morning.

Anyway, overtime was just as exciting as the game itself. Several lead changes, steals, dunks, foul troubles, rebounds, and with 54 seconds left, you still had no idea who was going to win. Of course, I was not to find out easily. With 54 seconds left, the extra time I had allowed for on the DVR ended, and in a sudden blink I was watching a re-run of Full House on Nickelodeon.

John Stamos has never made me more angry.

I went into panic mode. I hit "guide" on the remote and scrolled through the thousand or so channels we have trying to find ESPN. I couldn't find it or the category of sports channels. It was like they blinked out of existence and all turned into local news and horrible re-runs and cooking shows. I went back to where the game was recorded, and looked at the number of the channel. I punched in the numbers of the channel and got…the local news. Not even the sports.

Eventually, I read the play by play on Twitter found a highlight reel online which showed me what I missed. But it wasn't the same. The emotional roller coaster exhausted me. The whole next day I was out of whack because I stayed up past my bedtime doing something exciting.

There was a period in my life – most notably when I was at Duke and at the actual games live screaming my head of and jumping around for hours at a time like a lunatic – when I said things like, "Let's not go until 11 – nothing gets started until then" and had the deep sincere belief that anything more than three hours was a full night's sleep.

Not now. Nope. Less than 7 hours and I'm useless. I turn into a pumpkin somewhere around 9:45 most evenings. I'm too old for over-time. I guess if I want to keep my college degree, I'm going to have to move to the west coast so the late games start at 6:00.

Oh Christmas Tree

Being Jewish, I do not celebrate Christmas with my family. That said, living in sub-suburban Georgia, it is entirely impossible for me not to celebrate the Christmas holiday season in some form or fashion. Every organization has a Christmas party (very few of them are 'holiday' parties) and my children's public schools are decorated unapologetically for Christmas.

I'm not opposed to this, *per se*. I'm all about the joy of the season, and I'll celebrate anything that involves cookies and punch, and I'll celebrate twice if there is the possibility I'll get a gift. I think Christmas trees and lights are pretty and festive. I want to have a Merry Christmas, in the same way that I want all other 364 days of the year to be Merry. Merry = Good.

Somewhere in my house is a picture of my children with Santa, although to be fair, the random Santa we found at the Big Box Store looked vaguely alcoholic and a whole lot scrawnier than you'd want a jolly old elf to be. Instead of having a belly like a bowl fully of jelly he had a tummy like a sack full of rummy. Just saying.

I am glad that I don't have the burden of providing these things for my own family. Even considering ketchup as a vegetable, I can barely get it together to feed my family in a way that keeps away scurvy and rickets. The thought of clearing out the regular tchotchkes and replacing them with holiday tchotchkes and buying, setting up, and decorating a tree makes me panic. I have no earthly idea how people pull off that kind of labor. And that Elf on the Shelf? What a cute clever idea! But for real? Half the time at my house the tooth fairy gets hung up in traffic or doesn't think to have change for a twenty. There is no way the Elf could get into a different kind of mischief every night for a month, much less clean up the mischief from the day before. I'm still cleaning up my own mischief from last month, thank you very much. (No, seriously, as I write this in December, the centerpieces from my son's Bar Mitzvah on October 25th still sit in various stages of being taken apart on my living room floor.) Lately, I've seen marketed the Mensch on the Bench, which is a Jewishy version of the Elf. No thanks. Cute, but too derivative, and too much pressure.

Santa doesn't regularly come to our house, which isn't so much of a problem now that my kids are older, but it was a bit of a problem when they were younger and their teachers were using Santa as a disciplinary tool. ("If you don't stop, I'm going to tell Santa.....") I didn't want to undermine any method that would allow one grown person to keep control of twenty some-odd little ones, something I couldn't manage to do even if I were given possession of a drop down net, a pediatric cattle prod, and the voice of Mr. Rogers.

The first year my kids were aware of the problem, we were spending Christmas at the Lake, where there are no readily available shops nearby. Before we went to bed on Christmas Eve, my husband and I discussed whether or not we should do anything. We hunted around the house to see what we could find. In brown paper lunch sacks we placed a pack of Skittles and a dollar bill and wrote a note from Santa on the front saying that even though they didn't celebrate Christmas, he didn't want the Dufflets to feel totally ditched. Feeling left out of what everyone else is doing: that's the hardest part of the season for Jewish kids.

They were THRILLED with the Skittles and dollar bills. I set the bar low when they were young. That was some great serendipitous planning on my part.

I struggle with this 'typical mom' stuff, and I stand in amazement of people who manage to make it happen. I'm so bad that the other day I asked my kids if they wanted to make cookies with me, and they both looked at me as if they expected me to follow this unexpected burst of regular mommitude with an announcement of a fatal illness.

So, my hats off to you, Christmas-tree putter uppers and elf-assistants. You have accomplished something I could never in a million years pull off.

The Death of Southern Gentlemen, With a Side of Grrrrl Power

Seven million years ago, when I was learning how to drive, I asked my father how to check the oil in my car. Checking the oil was something I'd seen him do, and it seemed to me to be an Essential Part of Grown Up Car Ownership and Maintenance. My father's answer? "You pull into a full serve station and say, 'Will you please check the oil?'" That was the end of the subject.

Not long afterwards, I was driving with my father along the Meadowbrook Parkway on Long Island when the tire blew in the car. Dad told me to pull to the side of the road, which I did, and he proceeded to make me change my own tire. I remember what I was wearing: a khaki colored jumpsuit with enormous shoulder pads (it was the mid to late 80s and I was Very Fashionable) and short boots I thought of as Peter Pan boots. Not exactly the clothes you'd put on to do car maintenance, but I wasn't given a choice. I was not strong enough to turn the lug nuts with the crow bar, but Dad refused to help me beyond giving me advice and encouragement. Out of options, I braced myself on the side of the car and jumped on the crow bar until I loosened the lug nut. I felt like an absolute fool, jumping on the slender bar and trying not to fall, but by God I did it and I changed that tire myself on the side of the road. Rawr.

The difference between those two things is that there isn't any circumstance in which I will need to check the oil in order to get on my way, but there are plenty of circumstances in which I might need to change a tire.

I can't tell you the rush it was, the feeling like I could do anything in the whole world, including changing the tire on the side of the highway wearing impractical shoes.

Five million years ago, when I was auditioning future husbands in what seemed to be an endless run of first dates, that was one of my go-to questions. "Do you know how to change a tire?" If the answer was "no" or "You call AAA. Duh." – which was awfully, frighteningly often – there was no second date. And yes, I was questioning his essential manhood. Changing a tire is one of those life skills that every human living in the first world should know how to do.

Tonight I was sitting in the lobby of the Hugh Hodgson School of Music killing time while my son attended the Oboe and Bassoon Symposium. I was sitting in a sea of bored looking parents playing games on their phones and reading books. A woman came in the door and announced loudly, "Does anyone have jumper cables and know how to use them?"

I had jumper cables, and I know how to use them, however, I had no interest in getting out of my comfy chair and shutting down my computer to brave the cold wind to help a stranger. Still, no one else said anything in a reasonable amount of time, so I announced, "I do."

A man sitting across from me said, "Are you sure it is the battery? Does it go click click click or rawr rawr rawr click click click?"

Ah, I thought. This guy knows something about cars. He knows from the noises whether we are wasting time or not. Yay! Expert help.

"Just click click click. No rawr," she said.

"Then it's the battery," he said, and went back to reading his spy novel.

Despite the fact that we were in the Deep South, clearly there were no Southern Gentlemen in the room. I pushed my unladylike thoughts about the ungentlemanly behavior of this man and the other men in the room hiding behind books and tablet screens to the deep recesses of my brain. I had a Job to Do, what with no one else volunteering to do it, and all my concentration was spent on prayers that my memory of how to do this wouldn't result in a mushroom cloud-worthy explosion. I also allocated a small portion of my prayers to petitioning on behalf of this joker's wife/daughter/mother that none of them ever got stuck in a dark, cold parking lot with only another man like this one nearby.

I stuffed my computer in my bag and stood up to go outside. Together, my new friend Lynda and I drove my car to where her car was, dug under the shopping I had done earlier in the day, random jackets, reusable shopping bags, last week's gym clothes and the other assorted crapola that can generally be found in my trunk and found the jumper cables. It took me a minute to find the little latch thingie that opens my hood, and it took Lynda a minute to find the stick thingie that holds up her hood, but we eventually did what we needed to do, connected negative to negative and positive to positive and cranked 'er up. Yay us.

So, major props for my Dad for teaching me to be the kind of woman who doesn't need a man to come rescue her in a parking lot. And boo for the dozen or so men in the room who refused to be gentlemen and help us out. I'll make those two thoughts reconcile in my head somehow, someday.

Until then, "RAWR."

Surviving the Zombie Apocalypse

If you've read my first book, Mismatched Shoes and Upside Down Pizza, you know how much I loved the SkyMall catalog, with its can't-live-without merchandise like the fake grass and miniature-plastic fire hydrant indoor dog potty. When I found out SkyMall was no longer going to be published, I grieved. I don't mean, "Oh, that's too bad." I mean wracking sobs the likes of which hadn't been seen since I first saw Rose Tyler get trapped in an alternate universe in Dr. Who. I was sad. I was really really sad.

Until yesterday. Yesterday, the new Costco catalog came in the mail.

I wasn't really looking at the catalog, just kind of turning the pages to pass the time, waiting for it to get late enough to go to bed without shame. Blahblah, cheap mayonnaise, blahblah, fifty-five gallon drum of green peas, blahblah, pallet of toilet paper, blahblah. Then BLAMMO. The catalog page to end all catalog pages appeared.

It was the survivalist page.

For only $3,399.99 – DELIVERED!! – I could get 33,000 servings of freeze dried and dehydrated food, enough to feed a family of four for a year. I could also get a bucket with 180 servings of mac 'n' cheese. My daughter legitimately wants this – she got a dreamy look in her eye. "Is this," she began reverently, "just a big bucket of the noodles and you scoop out as much as you want and sprinkle the cheese on?"

"I guess so," I said, and, basing my opinion on the look on her face, made a mental note about what to get her when her birthday rolled around.

You could also get 80 servings of beef stroganoff with tender mushrooms for less than $100. Now, I have been known to actually cook beef stroganoff. I like it. But I've never dumped it out of a can, and unless I decide to start running a Victorian orphanage or a field Army base, I can't imagine why I would want that many giant cans of the stuff. Not even Oliver Twist would ask for more.

Of course, if you were going to eat that much freeze dried and dehydrated food, you'd need something to moisten and re-hydrate. I'd like to report that they sold a urine purification kit on the next page, but I can't. I'd like to report that somewhere in the catalogue was a still capable of rendering water potable or potato juice into vodka. But there wasn't that either. Just the food with a shelf life taking my children into middle age.

I'm just not that worried about a situation in which I might find a need for a year's worth of dehydrated food. Maybe I'm naïve, maybe my head is in the sand, or maybe I'm not paranoid enough. Or maybe, just maybe, I'm perfectly rational. I've read Cormack McCarthy's "The Road," Suzanne Collins' "The Hunger Games," and Veronica Roth's "Divergent." I've seen a few episodes of The Walking Dead. I think that makes me an expert on what a post-apocalyptic dystopian life would be. I think my family would be ok. My children both compete on the national level in archery, and my husband is more or less trained as a police sharpshooter. My son is a black belt, and my daughter is working on hers. All of which goes to show nothing at all, beyond that three out of four Duffs can aim and shoot in a purposeful direction, and maybe even take a punch, and probably could probably fend off a hoard of zombies for some time while we trap and eat squirrels and haul silty water out of the creek. We would probably survive the zombie apocalypse for a while if we wanted to.

But truly? If my days consist of eating dehydrated chicken & dumplings and recycled bodily fluids, I'm not sure I want to continue to provide fuel for my body. Of course, I've probably got six months of reserves on my bones, so oblivion would be a long time coming. Not only that, but given my family's inability to drive more than 15 minutes in a car together without someone melting down into tears, I'm pretty sure that if we were stuck in a bunker for more than a week we'd be plotting which one of us would get eaten first.

Oh well. It is time to put my head back in the sand. It is warm and comfortable there, and in that oblivion, all of the food is pre-moistened.

Leave Me Alone

I am not delusional. I know that I have "angry resting face." When I'm thinking, or submerged deep inside of my head, the (lack of) expression on my face looks irate. So. Given that premise, knowing that I look inherently grumpy, what is it about my face that makes people feel the need to interrupt me? Don't they fear the consequence?

On spring break, we went to visit my parents in Florida and, as you'd expect, we went to the beach. I like swimming, and I like the feel of the sand between my toes. I love that salty, sandy smell and the ever present hot breeze. One of my great pleasures – one which I refuse to call a guilty pleasure, because I feel no guilt about it whatsoever – is to sit on the beach with the background music of sea birds and surf, and read a book. Preferably one with no substance whatsoever.

We were at the beach, and I had a great, fluffy, and fun book to read, Jen Lancaster's "My Fair Lazy." While we were setting up the chairs and organizing the coolers, I could hear a small voice coming from my beach bag. "Read me! Reeeeeeeeeeeeeeeead me nooooowwwwww!"

"Soon, My Precious," I whispered. "Soon."

Finally, the kids deposited at water's edge and the old folks all sitting in beach chairs, I pulled out my book and opened it to my place. I read approximately three and a half sentences before the small talk began. It came from everyone. People I came with, children, random strangers. Ev. Ry. One.

I mean, seriously. If you see me sitting quietly reading a book, what would possess you to try to engage me in a conversation about the height (or lack thereof) of the waves, whether or not rain would make more interesting shells surface, or the blueness of the sky? If I wanted to chit chat, I would not have opened a book and begun to read it.

Frankly, even if I weren't reading a book, I wouldn't be terribly interested in a conversation about nothing in particular. I've never enjoyed or been the least bit good at small talk. It isn't that I don't know how to talk to people. I talk to people all day long. Unless they are lying to me, most people seem to like me. I'm just a big believer in the Zen saying, "Do not speak unless it improves the silence." Silence is not something that demands to be filled. Silence is whispery and elusive. It is something to be treasured and savored, because it is a precious and rare gift. Given the fact that I live with two children and a husband who revels in the retelling of stories that happened twenty years ago, it is a gift I rarely receive, but one I treasure more than chocolate.

I complain here about the day at the beach, because it was two days ago, but the truth is this happens more or less always. I make a point of never leaving home without something to read, just in case, because if I get five minutes of peace and quiet I'm going to take advantage. When I read my book in waiting rooms, the person next to me feels the need to tell me what they think of the doctor we are waiting to see. When I read on an airplane, my seatmate wants to know all about where I was and where I am going. Oddly enough, when I forget my book, or the battery on my Kindle dies, people are stone-faced and unfriendly. This is why I think it is something about the act of reading that inspires people to talk to me.

Even the people I feel comfortable being crabby in front of don't get the hint. Before I go to bed, the last step in my elaborate routine is to read a book. I cannot remember the last time I was able to lie down, open my book, read until I was finished, and then go to sleep. I think the cracking of the spine of a book, or maybe the sound of a page turning jogs the memory of my children. *Mooooooommmmm!! I need three dollars by tomorrow for the picnic! Mooooooommmmm!! Can you sign this?* My husband sees this final sign of my shutting down for the night and is reminded of all the things he wanted to say during the day but didn't. He asks me questions about the upcoming day or tells me things about the day that just finished. Sometimes it is something as simple as asking me to move over or where I put that credit card bill.

I think I speak for introverts everywhere when I say this: when we read a book (or write, or watch television, or pretty much do anything that doesn't require us to interact with other people) we are deeply inside of our heads. Honestly. When I'm in that zone, I often cannot hear or see what is immediately in front of me, so intense is my focus on what I am doing, or in exploring the labyrinth inside of my mind. It's like Sherlock Holmes' Mind Palace. When I am there and interrupted, I hear the sound of a record needle being dragged across the grooves, and I get a visual image of being grabbed by the scruff of my neck, my hair flowing forwards from the shift in momentum as I am yanked out of my own head. I am, in those moments, a three year old having a rainbow-sprinkled cupcake yanked out of her hand. Playdate's over, inner mind. Get out of the warm dreamy area, and come back into a reality that manages to be both harsh and boring at the same time.

So. Let this be a public service announcement. If you see me reading, don't begin non-emergency conversation with me. If I were in the mood to talk, I wouldn't have opened a book.

I Used To Be Smart

My son took the SAT the other day. He's only in Seventh Grade, but he took it for the Duke Talent Identification Program. His theory? I'm only in Seventh Grade. I'm not going to study. I want to just see how I do.

In some ways, I was ok with that. It really doesn't matter how he does, and he has enough mess on his plate that he doesn't need to add 'freaking out over the premature SAT' to the mix. Even if he bombed it, there was a 'no harm no foul' kind of thing going on, and he would have that experience to prepare him when he did it for real later in high school. I let it slide.

About a week before hand, I decided that he at least ought to look at some questions. I managed to find an "SAT Question of the Day" App for my phone, developed by the official College Board people, and free of charge. I think my son answered a total of three questions on it, but I became obsessed with it. I was surprised by how much I remembered – not so much the English and Reading questions, since I write for a living and read to live, but the math SAT practice questions. I was still able to do most of them, and the ones I got wrong, if I clicked on "explanation" then I remembered what I was supposed to have done. I was proud of me and my ever addling brain that I could still do this. Until two days before the SAT.

Then I stumbled on a math question that stumped me. The kicker was that I knew I was supposed to know it. It was like when you come up upon someone in the grocery store who gives you a great big hug and tells you they haven't seen you in ages and, oh my, you cut your hair, and did you ever marry that handsome helicopter pilot you were dating? You know from the bits of information and something pinging in the back of your brain that you are supposed to know this person, but you have absolutely no clue who they are, or even from what phase of your life they were unearthed. That's how I felt about this math question. It started with a big swoopy lowercase "f" and an "x" in parenthesis, which something told me meant "function," though function of what I could not tell you. (I pushed the rhyming but unhelpful Schoolhouse Rock song "Conjunction Junction" out of my head.) Somewhere else was "dx" over "dy," which I did remember had something to do with derivatives, though these days (and maybe then, too, I never really got higher math concepts deep in my gut) all I know is that when I read "Divergent" it seemed awfully derivative of "The Hunger Games." After that, I was stuck. There were some numbers, and some letters, and some basic math symbols like plus and minus signs. I stared at it, willing it to tell me even where to start.

So I did what I always do when I need an immediate answer to a question. I took a screen shot of it and posted it to Facebook. For good measure, and to speed the process, I tagged all my math and engineering and science friends that I could think of, noting proudly to myself that all the Professors in the STEM fields I could think of that were Facebook friends of mine were also women. The answers came pouring in. In the end, there were ninety-four comments, only about fifteen of which were me saying things like, "Hold up! You're assuming I remember how to solve a quadratic equation." It made me feel infinitely better that my friends who chose a career in science and math got it wrong some, and argued with each other about methodology. Even the Engineering Professor had to draw herself a picture to remember how to do it correctly. I appreciated the answer "purple" given by one friend, and the answer "banana" given by another. I was not alone. In the end, I understood it well enough to get the correct answer, though I never really understood what I was doing well enough to explain why it worked. Which, as I recall, is how I got through calculus the first (and second) go round and which cemented my conviction that despite the great wishes of my parents, I was not cut out for medical school.

So yeah, when my kids ask me why they have to learn this stuff that they know they will never use in the future, and they know they will forget within 45 minutes of the exam, my answer isn't some scripted parenting line that they will find it more useful than they think they will. My standard answer is something like, "it is the discipline of learning that is important, and teaching your brain to do things that it isn't naturally comfortable doing." But that's not the real answer. The real answer is this: I estimate I've forgotten 63.2% of everything I once knew. If I limited my knowledge to the things I cared about and wanted to remember, I'd forget 63.2% of those things, too. I need to pad my brain with useless information so I can go about forgetting that without regret.

In the meantime: have you seen my keys?

Yo Quiero Taco Bell

I have to admit that I spend a stupid amount of time at Taco Bell for someone my age. I associate Taco Bell with college road trips, when I could get a taco or bean burrito for the amount of change I could find in the sofa cushions. It's a little more expensive now, but, then again, it has been over a quarter century.

As it turns out, Taco Bell is currently the fashionable fast food for the younger teen set. Taco Bell is, as my daughter says, "bae.[1]" My children like it, and whenever we drive by one, which is more or less every time we leave the house, the younger Duffs beg to go. We leave the house a lot. Laundry piles up because I am rarely home long enough to accommodate the wash, rinse, spin, AND dry cycles on the appropriate machines. I give up and give in to fast food more than I should because, well, frankly, we need our food fast, and we need it on the way to karate from jazz band. Or was it from archery to Hebrew school. I can't keep track of the days, to be honest. I go where the calendar on my phone tells me to go when my phone tells me to go there.

Anyhoo, a few days ago we actually had something like 25 minutes in a row in which to eat, and the kids talked me into Taco Bell. Honestly, it is better now than it was back in the late 80s, and definitely better than a lot of fast food options. There are actual vegetables in some of the entrees. Precious little is fried. The presence of beans tells me that there might be a gram or two of fiber lurking underneath the tortillas.

We ordered whatever we ordered at the counter (not the drive thru! A great day!) and stood around waiting for our food. There were several bins with sauce packets, ranging in heat from mild to molten. On each packet was a short little saying. One said, "Live, Love, Tacos." Another said, "I'm spicy. Deal with it." Yet another said, "Will You Marry Me?"

---

1 For those of you over the age of 15, "bae" stands for "before anyone else" and it means best friend, boyfriend/girlfriend, or MVP of some kind.

I mean, I may be a Taco Bell apologist, and yo quiero Taco Bell more than I am proud of admitting, but I cannot imagine sitting at a Formica table with a hard plastic chair bolted into the ground and being overcome with both a romantic urge and a throat-tightening case of nerves, causing me to ask a life-altering question by way of passing a foil packet of mild sauce. What a story for your grandchildren. "Yes, Kawleigh-Flauer, (because by then the trend to name one's child by taking a perfectly normal noun and spelling it beyond recognition will have hit its peak) when your grandmother took a bite of her chicken Cantina burrito I was overcome by the way the fluorescent lights hit the sauce dripping down her chin. I loved her so much at that moment that I knew I wanted to spend the rest of my life with her, but I was so afraid that she'd say no that I couldn't speak. I saw the sauce packet, and gave it to her. She started to tear it open and pour it on her burrito, but I managed to croak out 'no' – and pointed to the message. She finished chewing, and then said yes. We framed the packet – it is over there on top of the old fashioned television set with an actual screen – and to this day the sauce is still in there, in the same way that our love is still in my heart."

Kawleigh-Flauer has been smiling and nodding because that's what he was told is polite, but he's actually listening to the iPod implanted in his head when he was a baby. This is 2055 or so, after all.

But I'm getting off topic. What I'd like to know is who writes these things, and what their title is, and how the job was advertised. "Wanted: copy writer to come up with pithy sayings to put on condiment packets." Is this an entry level position, or something you hope for a promotion into? Is there a writer's room like in a sitcom? Are there lists and lists of rejected packet-phrases? Who is in charge of deciding if the particular wording goes on a "Mild" or "Hot" or "Fire" packet? Does the guy who came up with "Live, Love, Tacos" paw through the bin for his contribution? Did he bring his Mom to Taco Bell to prove to her that he does so have a real job?

Looking back over what I've written here, I think it is pretty clear that even though I began by talking about how little time I have to eat a dinner more fancy than Taco Bell, I clearly have too much time to think. If you don't like it, though, "I'm spicy. Deal with it."

Grass is Stupid

I don't know why anyone bothers watching the weather this time of year. This is Atlanta. This is mid-July. I can say without any sort of doubt whatsoever, that it is going to be hot outside. Really hot. Convection oven hot. And humid, with air so thick you can cut it into slices and spread it on toast. Sometime in the afternoon, there might be a thunderstorm, which is the atmosphere's way of crying because it can't take the heat.

It was in this heat that my son and I set out to mow the lawn.

Our regular division of labor had me picking up sticks and gum tree balls and hickory nuts, and my son retrieving the lawn mower from the rickety shed held together with spider webs and song bird excrement. Jacob mowed the lawn, I picked up sticks. We drank lots and lots of water, and soaked our t-shirts with sweat. It was brutal work for us soft and squishy indoor people.

As I supervised the final passes of the front yard from my perch on the front stoop, watching the heat waves shimmer off the driveway, I had this epiphany: grass is stupid. Lawns are stupid. Mowing lawns in seven billion degree heat is even stupider.

I will grant you that a lush green lawn, freshly mowed and lined with flower beds can be very pretty. There is no better place to play a game of touch football, practice your cartwheels, or chase fireflies. However, for people like me, the number of times in a decade that I get a hankering to play touch football or put my feet over my head intentionally can be counted on one hand. One fingerless hand. And I'd just as soon watch the firefly show from the porch. So it seems silly to maintain grass for that purpose. I also want to point out that nowhere in my yard is a lush green lawn. It is mainly crabgrass and clover, with a few dandelions thrown in for good measure. If you mow it all down, however, it is a pretty consistent green and it looks nice, and does produce that fresh cut grass smell that is so wonderful they should make it into a car air freshener and is probably already a Yankee Candle.

So as I sat there, grateful for my teenage son who was finishing up the lawn, I wondered what we could do with that space that wouldn't require outdoor maintenance in the heat of summer. Most of our yard is wooded and natural, and I think that's beautiful. But there are patches of yard in the front and back of the house that could be altered in some way.

A wildflower garden would be nice, but that would only look good while the flowers were in bloom, and it would be difficult to separate the weeds from the flowers. A basketball court or tennis court would look weird, and besides, it would be too close to the house windows for people to be flinging balls at high velocities.

How about making it a beach? Filling the space with sand deep enough to build castles and sink an umbrella in. That would be nice while it lasted, but no doubt rain and gravity would erode it away pretty quickly.

Then I had the best idea. A gravel mosaic. It could be kind of like a Zen garden, and I could change the pattern with the seasons. Snowflakes in the winter. A great big sunflower in the summer. Maybe a clover for March. Then I thought about lifting large bags of gravel out of the trunk of my car and hauling them into the yard. That's work. Nope, one pattern fits all would have to work. Maybe some kind of compass rose or checkerboard pattern. Or maybe a great big spiral like the start of the yellow brick road. When weeds popped up, I could either yank them or spray them with toxic chemicals.

Meh, that's work, too.

I guess I'm stuck mowing the lawn for the foreseeable future. Or maybe shelling out another twenty so my son will pick up the sticks, too, or maybe Tom Sawyering his friends into helping. Or his sister.

Or me. I'm such a sucker.

Zero Dark Thirty

I went to sixth grade orientation last week. My actual sixth grader didn't go and wasn't oriented because she was still at camp. I admit that I did a pretty poor job of orienting myself, under the theory that I am not going to have to be able to find the classes, nor will I be able to help my daughter find the classes, and all the teachers are the same ones my son had two years ago so I don't need to meet them. The school is a brand new school that still smells like paint, so everyone, including teachers, will be lost the first few days anyway.

I did find out that my daughter's bus will pick her up at 6:03 a.m. Not 6:02, not 6:04, but 6:03. Of course, based on my experience with putting children on public school buses for the eight years prior to this year, the actual time will be anywhere from 5:50 a.m. and 6:20, probably closer to 6:30 on the first day.

I'm guessing that most of you who are reading this have never met my daughter or, if you have, you have never laid eyes on her at a time that begins with the number six. For that matter, I have hardly ever laid eyes on her that early, at least not in recent years, and I have the parental right to barge into her room whenever I want. Of course, I don't want to barge in anywhere at 6:00 a.m. I don't want to be anywhere but in bed that early. I only want to have theoretical knowledge that 6:00 a.m. is a thing. I don't want to have witnessed it my own self.

My daughter? Way worse than me when it comes to mornings. As far as she's concerned, it is inhuman to require her to speak or interact or roll out of bed any time before noon. I have no idea how I'm going to get her out of bed in time to be at the end of the driveway at 6. Especially since her brother, who wakes up chipper and chatty, will be, and I quote, "hogging the bathroom." I'm thinking it might be easier to just let her stay up until it is time to go to school, and then let her nap in the afternoon. I think she could handle that better.

All of which raises the question: why, in a world basically structured around 9 to 5, did anyone think it was a good idea for teenagers to start functioning intellectually at 7:25 am, or whatever off beat time it is that school actually starts. Anyone who has ever been a teenager or interacted with a teenager or watched more than 5 minutes of television knows that teenagers can't do anything that requires thought beyond "socks go on feet; head goes through the neck hole of the shirt" early in the morning. I can't believe that the kids wouldn't learn more if they could start learning at 10:00 a.m. instead.

And, more to the point, as if raising two children so thick in the middle of puberty that you can smell the Clearasil from three blocks away wasn't difficult enough, I am going to have to start getting up at 5:00 a.m. just to supervise the whole mess and ensure compliance. Which means that if I want the 8 hours of sleep I'm told is required to get in order to be well rested and fully functional, I'm going to have to go to bed at 9:00 p.m. I'm not even HOME by 9:00 p.m. some days. And if I EVER want to watch the end of a ballgame, I'm not going to be able to get enough sleep.

Now, I know that I'm not nearly the only one in this boat, and that teachers have to get up that early every day no matter what. I'm just wondering if anyone actually thought about that before making this insane schedule.

But back to my daughter: how exactly I am going to force her out of bed at 5:00 a.m. is a mystery for the ages. I may resort to a bucket of ice, air horns, or physically dragging her. I don't think that taking away her iPhone is going to work, because in order for a threat to be effective, she'd have to be capable of higher order thinking: understanding the concept of future payment for current behavior, and being able to properly order her values/wants – what is more important? The phone or 5 more minutes of sleep? She's not awake enough to understand cause and effect, or even to recognize the pointlessness or arguing about it.

Resistance is futile, little girl. Get used to it.

Meanwhile, for realsies and for seriousness, if anyone has any ideas or tried and true methods for getting a night owl moving in the early morning, I'm all ears: send me an email.

> *Note: at the time I put this book together, we were nearly through the school year in question. Sometime around Thanksgiving I just gave up and decided to drive them to school every morning. We all get to sleep an hour more this way, and I've somehow convinced myself that I like getting to the office at 7:30 in the morning when it is quiet and the phones don't ring. It's amazing what the human mind can do to protect itself from reality.*

Basic Competence

I've done the math, and assuming my calculations are correct (which you should not assume if you believe math should only be done by trained professionals, or at least people who regularly add 7+5 and get 12 every time) I spend 73.8% of every day trying to get other grownups to do what they are supposed to do. Of the remaining 26.2% of my day, 23% is trying to get my kids to do what they are supposed to do, and 3.2% involves coffee. Coffee always does what it is supposed to do, and it does so pleasantly.

I promise you that I don't expect or really want anyone to go above and beyond. If someone goes above and beyond, it only makes me feel like a slacker. Which I might be, but I don't want to feel that way. So just do what you are supposed to do and be done with it.

This seems like such an incredibly low standard that it should be met with some regularity. But it isn't. Sure, I prefer things the way I prefer them, but I know that D is for Done and that's all I want. I'm not a neat freak, I'm not a Type-A Nut Job, I'm not especially anal retentive (the prunes have helped), but I do have standards. Low ones, but standards nonetheless.

For example, the rest of the house may look like the Crips and Bloods had it out once and for all in my living room, but I want my kitchen and bathroom clean. The places with running water. The places where I eat and where I make myself and my various parts clean. And yet.....and yet.....my one hard and fast rule is that when I get home from work there shouldn't be breakfast dishes in the sink. There is a retired adult in my house and two children who, while they will always be my babies, are five foot five and five foot nine respectively. Everyone can reach as high and as far back as I can reach. Therefore, between the three of them you'd think someone would rinse out a cereal bowl from time to time and fling it in the dishwasher.

You'd think wrong.

I'm the only one who seems to be even vaguely aware of the mildew that grows in the toilet, sometimes to the point where it has begun to evolve into a sentient being capable of starring in its own reality show. I think this is a vision thing. Like color blind people can't tell red from green, my family members can't tell dirty from clean. No, the kitchen isn't clean if there are still crumbs on the counter. No, the bathroom isn't clean if there is enough hair on the floor to gather up and knit a sweater with. (Yes, I know I ended that sentence with a preposition. Get over your pedantic self.)

I wish it were all as easily fixable as swiping a paper towel across a countertop and swirling a brush in a toilet bowl. If the problem were only cleaning and only my family, I could fix it. (Maybe?)

Nope. The problem is so much larger than people who share my last name. Getting people to show up for appointments is a problem. Getting people to respond to important questions is a problem. Getting people to return phone calls is virtually impossible. So many times at work I am asked a question that begins, "When will……..?" This makes my hair curl. When will anything? Couldn't tell you. I can tell you when I will do something, but that's where my control and knowledge ends. My crystal ball is broken, and the best I can do is tell you when another grownup should do something, not when they will. Sometimes I can't even get people to respond when their response means that I will give them money. It is ten times as hard when I need someone to do something that doesn't get them any money or – gasp – might cost them something.

We're all human, I know, and we all do what we can to get through the day. Sometimes things slip through the cracks, sometimes we forget, and sometimes something more important comes along. But how long does it take to shoot an email that says, "I haven't forgotten you, I just got swamped?"

I'm a doer. I like getting things done. I don't mind working, and I live for the feeling of accomplishment that comes from the pride of a completed task. I cannot bear the inability to complete a task because of a failure on someone else's part to hear the Call of Duty. The only thing that prevents me from a full screaming banshee tantrum including the clawing-out-of-eyeballs-of-the-offender(s) is an enormous amount of self-control.

To paraphrase Leviticus, do not curse the deaf or put a stumbling block in front of the blind, nor shall you fail to do what you need to do so that others can get stuff done. To paraphrase the Serenity Prayer, God grant me the serenity to accept the things I cannot control; the strength (and stamina) to control the things I can; and the wisdom not to send death threats to those whose inability to act responsibly gets in my way.

Misophonia

I've never been much of a gum chewer. As someone who has teeth removed and orthodontia to fix Temporomandibular Joint Disorder (TMJ), I'm lazy and not a huge fan of exercising those (or any) muscles unnecessarily. (Especially when there are so many wonderfully necessary uses for those muscles, such as eating pie.) Plus, gum loses its flavor quickly for me, and tastes sour after mere minutes.

I am in the minority. Most people I know have a pack of gum within arm's reach of any chair in which they regularly sit. I'm always being offered gum. I always refuse. So what, right?

I'll tell you what. I cannot bear the sound of someone else chewing gum. It is such a wet, sloggy, sticky sound. The moist, clicky noises don't only make me sick to my stomach. They create a visceral, almost violent reaction. I feel like my head is being pelted with spitballs, and I become filled with a blind, uncontrollable rage. I say uncontrollable, but I – almost – always control it, at least outwardly. But the shouting in my head, which peppers words like "cud" and "disgusting" and "heifer" with words decidedly more peppery, drowns out all dignified and rational thought.

I have actually had this thought flit through my brain: "If you don't stop chewing that gum like you've just coughed it up from your fourth stomach I will drive this minivan directly into that tanker truck in front of us, see if I won't."

Since I'm American, I consider every thought that isn't comprised of sunshine and rainbows and optimism (and some thoughts that are too sunshiny and rainbowy and optimistic) as a diagnosable disorder. This particular diagnosable disorder is Misophonia which, according to Wikipedia literally means "hatred of sound" in which negative emotions are triggered by specific sounds. The sound of gum chewing is specifically listed as a trigger. So, without the necessity of finding a Misophonia specialist and being subjected to a battery of tests which require me to (I'm assuming) color within the lines using pastel colors while listening to a nine year old cram an entire pack of Big League Chew in his mouth, I'll go ahead and diagnose myself.

I say nine year old and Big League Chew in that paragraph there, because it sounded funny to me. But the truth is that the worst gum chewers seem to be the oldest gum chewers, and the more closely they are related to me the worse my Misophonia sends red lightning bolts to cloud my retinas and judgment. Maybe Nicorette gum just sounds worse than Hubba Bubba. Or maybe baby teeth don't make the same sloshy, goopy sounds when unsticking themselves from gum as their crowned, be-fillinged elders do. Or maybe older folks hear worse and can't self-regulate the racket they are making because they can't hear it to know it is happening.

Dunno, don't care, and I've got a whole Wikipedia page with 23 footnotes citing actual believable legitimately medical-sounding sources like the "Journal of Clinical Psychology" saying I'm not alone.

Battle for Control

There are certain kinds of battles that certain kinds of people are always going to lose. Every single time.

Let's say there are two families who go to the beach. The Smith family wants to enjoy the smell of the salt air and the sounds of the surf, swim, build sand castles, and read books in the sun. The Jones family wants to listen to music and dance in the sand and enjoy a good cigar. The Jones family is going to get its way. The Smith family is going to have to listen to the Joneses' music and smell their cigars and will get no peace and quiet. Every time.

Late people always win, too. Let's say two people are trying to go to the movies. Jane likes to get there early, buy her tickets and her popcorn, and have her choice of seats while the lights are still on. John likes to cruise in halfway through the opening credits. John will win this battle. Every time.

Same goes for messy people. If you have to share a workspace with someone, and you are neat and they are messy, your workspace will be messy. Every time.

As someone who likes quiet and fresh air, neat, organized spaces, and being places on time, I feel like I always lose and, frankly, I'm getting tired of it. I've spent a lot of time thinking about why I always have to be the loser and the answer is because when I do what I want – be quiet and stink-free and neat and show up on time – it doesn't affect anyone else. When the noisy and smoky and late people do what they want, I have to hear, smell, and wait for them. If we all just go about our respective businesses, I am going to lose. Ok, don't call it lose: they will get their way and I will get their way. Does that sound less whiny?

The older I get the less I'm sure I care about how whiny I sound. At what point in my life do I get to declare that I have paid my dues and other people should defer to my will? I'm saying it is at this point in my life. So listen up, people, and yes, I am talking to a large number of my family members, extended, virtual, and otherwise. I'm gonna list a few things that you do that annoy the bejeebers out of me, and which I have been putting up with for nearly five decades. It's my turn, and you will stop doing these things simply because you love me and you want me to be happy.

Don't chew gum in my presence. I wrote a whole chapter about about how I hate this, and I know you read it, and yet I still spent the better part of a ten hour car ride listening to the sounds of regurgitated cud.

1. I hate the smell of cigarette smoke. It is a migraine trigger for me. It makes the entire time I have to smell it unpleasant. If you must smoke because your nicotine addiction is that strong, kindly go somewhere else and no, I don't care if it is cold out or raining out. I will not coddle your addiction.
2. I think it was Buddha, or maybe someone else unquestionably wise, who said, "Don't speak unless it improves the silence." Consider your audience before you speak: does this person appear interested in how a fuel line is connected from one place to another in a Yamaha jet ski? Is this person truly concerned about the family history of someone she's only met once and will probably never meet again? If not, be quiet.
3. Relatedly, quiet is ok. Silence is ok. Silence is, actually, more than ok. I get that I'm an introvert, and I need time wandering around my head in order to process all the information I've received since the last head-wander, but I honestly don't know how anyone can say anything thoughtful about anything if you haven't shut up long enough in the past however long in order to actually have thoughts about what you are going to say. Silence does not beg to be filled. It begs to be appreciated.
4. If I am reading a book, and you have something important to say, wait until I'm done reading or acknowledge your presence

on my own. The only exceptions would be the phrases "the house is on fire," "a bear just broke down the front door and is demanding honey," and "my sister fell down and I'm not sure her leg should be pointing that way." Everything else can wait until the chapter is finished.

5. If we have agreed on a time to go somewhere, and it is that time, excepting in the case of an intestinal emergency, it is time to go. If you don't have your hair fixed or your favorite jacket found, tough noogies. We are going when I say it is time to go.

These requests seem reasonable to me, and they all turn around a simple theme: leave me alone unless you have something interesting to say, do what you are supposed to do, and don't force me to listen to your crappy music or your smell your unfiltered Camels.

Now that I think about it (having had a rare moment of silence in which to do so), most of my problems could be solved by my use of a human hamster ball. Surely they sell those somewhere?

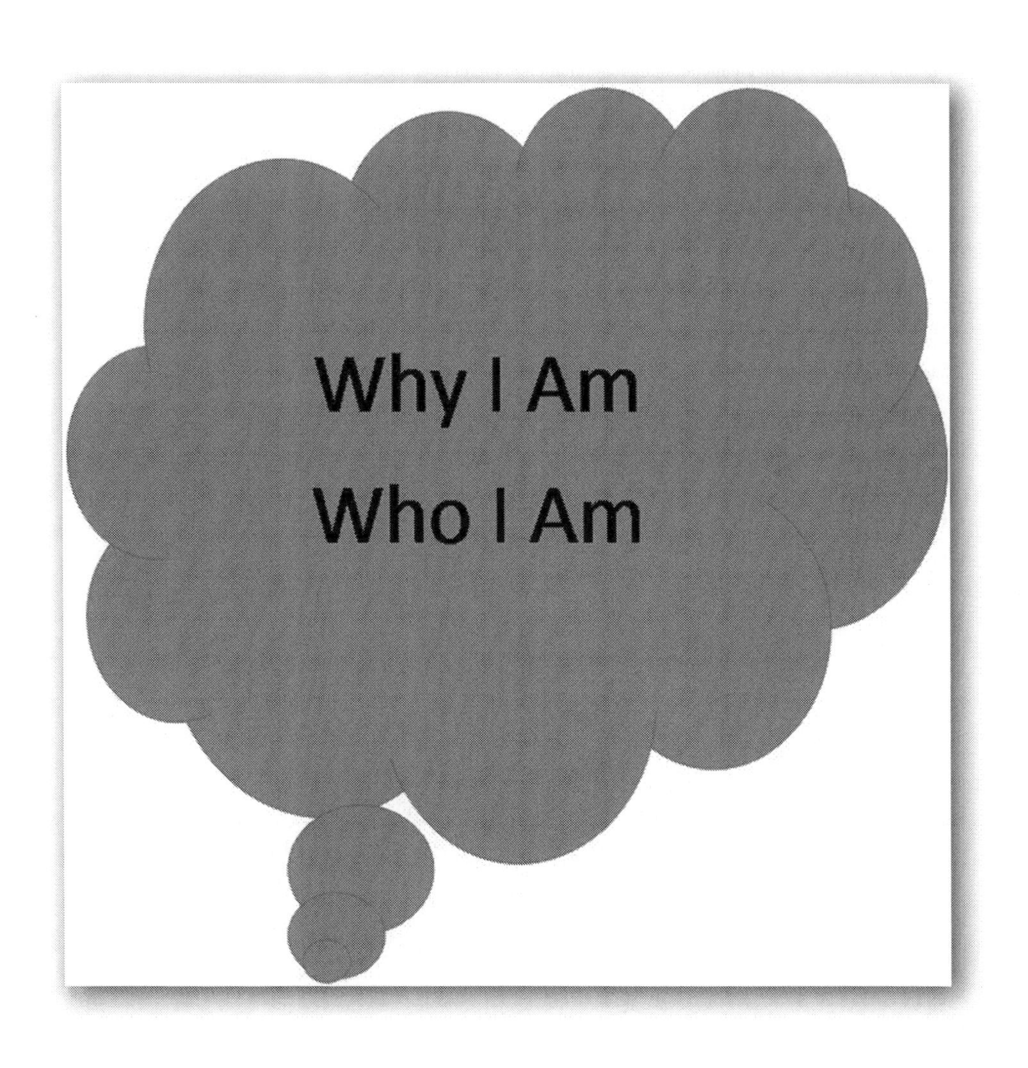
Why I Am
Who I Am

Why I Am Who I Am

The Great Guitar Saga

My mother's mother's sister, Aunt Pearl, had an old guitar that used to belong to her son, Jeffrey. Aunt Pearl kindly wanted to give this guitar to my daughter. Aunt Pearl, an admirably independent nonagenarian, lives alone in a two story house near the beach in New York, and, if you had to pick a celebrity she resembled the most, you'd pick George Costanza's mother on Seinfeld. If you can, to make this story better, hold that voice in your head while reading Aunt Pearl's lines.

It is no small task getting a guitar from Long Island to Georgia. The logical courier was my mother, who lived on the opposite end of the country, in South Florida, where you'd expect a retired Jew to live. Over the summer, my mother went to visit (among others) Aunt Pearl, and took the guitar in order to bring it to me.

Only she didn't. She left it at my sister's house, for reasons unknown and unknowable, but were best described as "Ah, what a pain in the *tuchus* to bring it on the plane. I'll get it when we drive up next time."

It was my mother's fault, then, that Marin didn't get the guitar.

Except that no one told Aunt Pearl that Marin didn't get the guitar, and so she developed a(n understandable under the circumstances) grudge against my daughter for not writing a thank you note for the guitar she didn't get, and me by association, because as her mother it was my job to ensure that the proper thank you note was written.

So, it was my fault that Marin didn't write the thank you note.

My mother called me, exerting all that thickly-accented aggressive Yankee Jewish Guilt through the phone lines. "Can'tcha just write Aunt Pearl a note saying how much ya like the gitaah? Would it killya to make an old woman happy?"

So I wrote a note to Aunt Pearl. I told her, sincerely, how sweet she was to remember my children in this way, how much my son loved the guitar she gave him several years ago, and how excited my daughter was to get a legacy of her own. I thought it was a nice note. I really did. I was proud that nothing was my fault any longer, nor was my daughter thought to be inconsiderate.

I was right about my daughter, but apparently I was still on the hook. A few days later, I got a call from my mother. She was hot. "Whydja write that note to Aunt Pearl? You were supposed to write it AS Marin and say you already got the gitaah. Now she knows I didn't give it to you. Huh? Are you afraid to lie? Sometimes lies are good, ya know. They make other people feel bettah. I'm gonna killya." Ah yes, expressing powerful feelings. That's how my family says, "I love you."

It wasn't until my mother inhaled a deep lungful of cigarette smoke and blew it out so forcefully I could practically smell it from 600 miles away that I was able to assert my, "But I didn't know I was supposed to lie!" defense, which fell, somewhat literally, on deaf ears.

And, it was back to being my fault.

Then Aunt Pearl called me to tell me that my mother was "Nuts" and there was no reason she couldn't take the guitar on the plane, and all this time she was mad at Marin but she shouldn't have been, because it was my mother's fault all along for leaving the guitar at my sister's house.

I called my mother to tell her the whole thing was back to being her fault. After denying it, my mother made a strangled frustrated noise. "Ah, my cigarette rolling machine just jammed up."

This unexpected conversational segue intrigued me. "Why are you rolling your own cigarettes? Are you growing your own tobacco?"

"Ha ha," she said. "Very funny. I'm doing it to save thoity bucks a cawtin. Your kids should be doing this fuh me."

"Mom, at no point in my lifetime are my children rolling your cigarettes for you."

I heard another deep drag of a cigarette, the squeak squeak squeak of the rolling machine, and a bad word as it jammed again. "You never know when a skill like that will come in handy. I just wish they'd legalize marijuana so I could go into business."

I love my parents dearly, but there's a reason I live so far away.

The next day Aunt Pearl called me up to tell me the conclusion of her investigation into the Great Guitar Caper. My sister had thoughtfully brought the guitar to Georgia in October when she came down for my son's Bar Mitzvah. My father picked her up at the airport, loaded the guitar in the back of his trunk, and promptly forgot about it until he was unpacking his trunk back at home. He found the guitar, and put it on a shelf in the garage, telling no one until directly asked that very day.

So, in the end, it was, is, and always will be HIS fault.

I'm just glad it isn't mine anymore. I can't handle the pressure. It's stressful enough just being a part of the conversation.

Camp Grandma

My Mom is not that old, considering how old I am and how old her grandchildren are. I won't tell you how old she is, for fear that she reads this and cuts me out of the will, but suffice it to say that it has not yet been a decade since she threw herself a toga party to celebrate her first Social Security check. (Seriously.)

My Mom is a tightly wound ball of creative energy. She is incapable of sitting still. Despite the six or so decades between her age and my children's, the Dufflets have trouble keeping up with her. Anyone who can't keep up with her, which is everyone, is immediately designated "lazy" or "boring" or, worse, "not helpful."

My Mom is the woman Pinterest was designed for. She happily spends hours searching things like "Recycled Garden Art" and then pins them to her wall, only to be unable to ever find the pins again because she doesn't entirely know how to work her computer. But she will call me and tell me to look at her Pinterest account to see what she pinned because she needs me to save the raw materials for the projects.

Mom is convinced that the only things you should buy for arts and crafts projects are glue and paint, with the occasional ball of twine thrown in for good measure. And you'd better have a 60% off coupon for Joann's when you go in there, because the idea of paying full retail is as repugnant to her as broccoli is to your average toddler. Everything else should come from your recycling bin. Or your neighbor's recycling bin (picked through after dark with a flashlight.) Or a nearby dumpster. Or, if she's lucky and can convince my father to stop the car, the side of the highway.

This past week, my parents came up to Georgia from Florida for their annual summer pilgrimage to see their grandchildren. I had been instructed to save plastic bottles, especially the colored ones like laundry detergent bottles, lids of all kinds, soda cans, plastic spoons, and egg cartons. By the time my parents arrived, I had several garbage bags full. (p.s. I didn't save enough to prevent my mother from convincing a friend of mine to take her to the dump to get more cans.)

Within ten minutes of her arrival, Camp Grandma was open for the season. It begun with a demonstration of what we were to make as well as a Pinterest slide show. She had roses made of the bowls of plastic spoons, pigs made of milk bottles, and wild daisies made of Arizona Iced Tea cans. She had rebar to make totem poles.

Under the theory that my mother raised me just fine, and loved my children too much to let any harm come to them, I excused myself and let the kids enjoy themselves at camp. It was only ten minutes before my son came to me with a bloody paper towel pressed to his hand and a grin on his face. "Mom!" He said. "Look at the flower I made out of a Coke can! And I only lost a pint of blood."

Any thought that I might actually get work done while the kids were occupied was quickly dispelled. I was sent on regular missions to get various sizes of bandages, candles, shopping bags of different colors, Elmer's glue, paper plates, fishing line, and told to continue to drink Arizona iced tea since both the cans and bottles were ideal for projects.

The intensity was impressive. They made a garden of flowers out of sticks, soda cans, and plastic lids. They made a totem pole of pigs. They made a bit of abstract art we're calling "Sputnik" and a wind sock of sorts. They made an impressive mess and used several bottles of paint.

Most of all, they made memories. My Mom is getting older and, while she isn't slowing down and hasn't quit smoking, her health fails little by little. Her back hurts. She has a nasty permanent cough. She's partially blinded from a stroke, and has about seven million stents in her heart. She's not going to be around forever, but while she's here, she's setting one heck of an example. Don't let handicaps stop you from having fun. Don't let a few cuts on your fingers affect the finished project. And, most importantly, choose your laundry detergent based upon the color of the bottle.

My Own Personal Summer

There is a joke we tell in these parts so often that it couldn't possibly be funny anymore: if you don't like the weather, you should just wait 15 minutes. Such is spring in Georgia. It is not uncommon for there to be a forty degree swing in temperature between eight in the morning and three in the afternoon. And the warmer temperature might be the one in the morning. Or, it might stay at whatever cool temperature you find when you wake up. There is no way to tell. A random monkey throwing darts would get it right more often than the local meteorologists. In April, for example, I never know how to dress. A light sweater? A tank top? A filmy skirt? Thick pants? Full coverage shoes or sandals?

The other morning, I woke up at a time when most college students are going to bed in order to cook my son an actual breakfast before he met the school bus at 6:20 in the morning. It was a semi-special occasion, the first day of the year end high pressure Georgia Milestones test upon which, to hear my children say it, the fate of the universe rests. I took a shower and, based on the weather the day before, a most unreliable method, I put on pants and a cotton sweater.

After my son walked down our driveway to meet the bus, I realized he had left the phone on the counter. He needed it, since his actually getting home that day required some parental coordination. I stepped out on the front porch into the opening scene of a horror movie.

There wasn't anything grisly, this was the opening scene of the movie: the one where everything looks so calm and peaceful except for the creepy music. My eyes did their uncaffeinated best to readjust from the inside halogen lights. As it was, they hadn't yet given me the ability to see in the dark. I could see very little in the moonless morning. I heard the wind moving the tree branches. Night bird calls shrieked over the rooster's constant call from next door. (An aside: how that rooster, which hasn't shut up in five years, morning, noon, or night, hasn't either gone hoarse or ended up a pile of feathers is beyond my understanding.) My house is in the middle of the woods. The driveway is curved and about a hundred yards long. I could not tell if my son was still there or if the bus had come already.

"Jacob?" I called out. A few blinks of a flashlight answered me.

I started to make my way down the driveway. The sun wasn't out yet, but it was hot and muggy. It was so dark that I wasn't really sure if I was walking on the driveway or on the hard packed dirt on the side of the driveway. I had a vague sense of where the road was and headed in that direction. I handed Jacob the phone, and stayed with him for the next minute or so until the bus came. As soon as it started coming, I crept back into the darkness so the other middle schoolers on the bus wouldn't see me – I might take pride in my ability to embarrass my kids, but even I have limits.

I walked back up the driveway and in the house, feeling the sweat on the back of my neck dampening my hair. If it was this hot at zero-dark-thirty in the morning, it was going to be a scorcher of a day. Given the thermostat wars in my office (I often have to turn the air DOWN to 75 degrees) I didn't want to take a chance at a hot, sweaty (read: stinky) day. I pulled off the sweater and put on a gauzy, short sleeved shirt. I swapped my ballet flats out for sandals.

And proceeded to freeze the rest of the day. For the rest of the universe, it was a blustery, grey, fifty-two degree day. It was summer for me and only me, a personal summer, and perhaps some other middle aged sisters, and only summer for about forty five minutes, just long enough for me to get far enough away from my house to regret my choices and not be able to do anything about it.

I'm not sad to have reached this time in my life. My family is complete, and menopause is, if nothing else, free, natural birth control. My metabolism has already come to a screeching halt, and bizarre grey hairs sprout from unusual places. This is the next logical step, and I welcome it with open arms.

Open arms and cardigans over tank tops, that is. Layers are the middle aged woman's friend.

I know that now.

Chicken Soup for the Sick

The seasons are changing now, from summer to fall, from eyeball melting heat to mere hotness, and here in Georgia that means that on any given day it might be 85 degrees out or 50. Or both.

This is a recipe for illness in the Duff household, with my son and me generally bearing the brunt of the sniffles. This year it nailed my daughter as well.

So I made chicken soup. As a purebred Jewish mother, continuing an unbroken line of Jewish mothers going back to Sarah, Rebecca, Rachel, and Leah, I make a mean chicken soup, and it cures all manner of mental and physical illnesses. It is, to repeat a stereotype, Jewish Penicillin. As a public service, I am going to share the recipe here, in narrative form, so pay attention as there is no convenient list of ingredients. Things are measured in the traditional manner: in terms of "a bunch" or "some," so be careful.

The first thing you need to do is make sure that you are going to be home for at least six hours. This is not something you can do in a crock pot, and you have to cook it for absolute ever for it to be any good, and we all know you can't leave the house with the stove on or there will be a fire and you will burn up and die along with all your family heirlooms. You also need a giant soup pot, the bigger the better. A cauldron would work, if you have one.

Put a whole bunch of water in the pot. Then put a whole chicken, all cut up in the pot. I mean the whole chicken. Don't take any of the skin or fat off. Put in the nasty bits that they put in the paper bag, like the gizzard and heart. (Not the paper bag, though.) Everything but the feathers and beak, really, and probably the beak would be ok, but the feathers would ultimately get caught between your teeth.

Get one of those normal sized bags of carrots, and peel them all, and cut them into large chunks. Throw the chunks in the soup pot. Then get a bunch of celery (what is a grouping of celery called? You know, the amount that all grows together from one root – is it a bunch of celery? A pride of celery? A murder of celery?) and cut it into chunks and throw it into the pot as well.

Get two or three turnips (depending on how big they are and whether or not you like turnips) and half-heartedly cut the skin off and chunk them and throw them in the pot, too. You can put whatever root vegetables look good. I've used rutabaga and parsnips, though I prefer the turnips.

Take a whole lot of fresh dill, and either wrap a rubber band around it or stuff it into this funky cool silicone thing I got from Pampered Chef which lets you stuff the herbs and things you want to flavor the soup in it without getting the actual leaves and resulting green sludge all over the food, and then throw that in the pot as well.

If you want to, you can add salt and if you really want to you can add pepper, though I wouldn't recommend it.

And that's all. After it boils, reduce it to a simmer and cover it. Once it has cooked for four or five hours minimum (more if you can stand it) fish out the dill and the nasty chicken bits and serve. If you want to go full on authentic, you can buy a canister of Manischewitz matzoh meal and follow the recipe on the side for matzoh balls, though honestly if you want any at all you are going to have to triple or quadruple it. If you want to go just passibly authentic, get skinny egg noodles and put them in the soup.

I take out all the chicken and, after it has cooled, I separate out the bone and gristle and icky parts and use the meat to make chicken salad. I make one heck of a chicken salad, both literally and metaphorically. And that's what this whole thing is, isn't it? An excuse to do the thing I was put on this Earth to do: take care of my babies, and express my love in my favorite love language, that is, food. Chicken soup, like Mommies, nurtures, nourishes, heals, and gives us what we need to live. And the parts you would throw out, the overboiled, mushy, gross looking parts, a Mommy can make them into something that works great on rye bread or Triscuits.

That's one of the many things Mommies are good at, or at least this particular Mommy. Making chicken soup and chicken salad.

What Comes Around

Everything old is new again, they say, and just like you can actually find legwarmers for sale, and real live fashionable teenagers wearing them, other 80's things are making a comeback.

After we decided that earrings were a no-go for my son's birthday, Jacob decided he wanted an old school turntable to play records on, not that he owned any records, but he heard that records sound better, and some artists are releasing albums on vinyl and he wants to get them. What comes around keeps on going around, mostly at 33 1/3 rpm. Ha ha.

So, I bought him a turntable. I bought him one with USB ports and auxiliary doodads so he could hook it up to his iPhone or computer or whatever, and theoretically you can copy the tracks somehow, which I thought might be useful. I gave it to him the morning of his birthday, and he was excited, even if he didn't have any records to play.

On his request, I went into the basement and did an archeological expedition in the vast strata of detritus in order to find my old record collection. I grabbed a handful, including some 45's, and brought them upstairs.

My son is a teenager, 5'9", with a very low voice, and he looks very manly. Therefore, I forget that there are some things I consider basic that he didn't know how to do.

When my children were babies and I was new to this whole mothering thing, I was shocked to find out how much they didn't know. That was one of my favorite parts of parenting, watching these little fleshy lumps become fully formed people who could, with my instruction, drink from a straw, use a spoon, and find their own toes on command.

When my son was six weeks old, he got a cold. He wasn't terribly sick, as far as illness goes, but his little body wasn't equipped to handle a stuffy nose. He had no idea that he could breathe through his mouth on purpose, and didn't have the fine motor control to sniff or blow his nose on command. So he would try to breathe through his nose, find himself unable to breathe, panic, and then cry, which made him breathe through his mouth. He'd realize he was breathing again, settle down, then close his mouth, make a weird snuffling sound as he tried to breathe through his nose, and then the cycle would repeat. I'm the kind of mean parent that thought it was hilarious and videotaped it, but I used the booger sucker thing as best I could, and somehow he lived another fourteen plus years.

That's what I thought of when I handed Jacob my vintage Duran Duran "Rio" record and he looked at it, and then the turntable, and had no idea how to put the two of them together to make music. I told him to put the hole in the record on the pokey thing, which he did fairly easily. He didn't know what to do next, and I found myself explaining the concept of the spiral and the needle and how the whole trick was to not make that skrrrrritch sound because that would scratch the record, and I've managed to go since 1982 without scratching up "Hungry Like the Wolf" and I might be justified in killing him if he did it now.

By the way? Turns out that vintage copies of Rio are only worth about 5 bucks on EBay. I guess most 80's girls kept theirs and there are a lot on the market.

Also? Pink Floyd's "The Wall" is mostly moody and depressing.

I explained that going all the way to the record store and buying 45's was what we did instead of instantly downloading singles from iTunes when a song came out. I told him that I was not to be judged by my collection of 45's, which included Phil Collins' "Against All Odds" and "Let's Hear It For The Boy" by Deniece Williams, but, rather, to be applauded for still having one of those plastic thingies you needed to fit a 45 on the spindle still wedged firmly in a record.

He also learned that playing a 33 rpm record at 45 rpm and vice versa is good for a few laughs.

I learned that "Footloose" still makes me want to dance. And that my dancing is a different kind of embarrassing than it was in 1984. Also, I care less, and danced anyway, even under threat of a video being posted on the internet. You can't shame me. I'm a mom.

And turns out? My son actually liked some of my ancient records and I hear him listening to them when I am not in the room.

We did know how to have fun back then, and music is still music and can still move us together, even if we are decades apart.

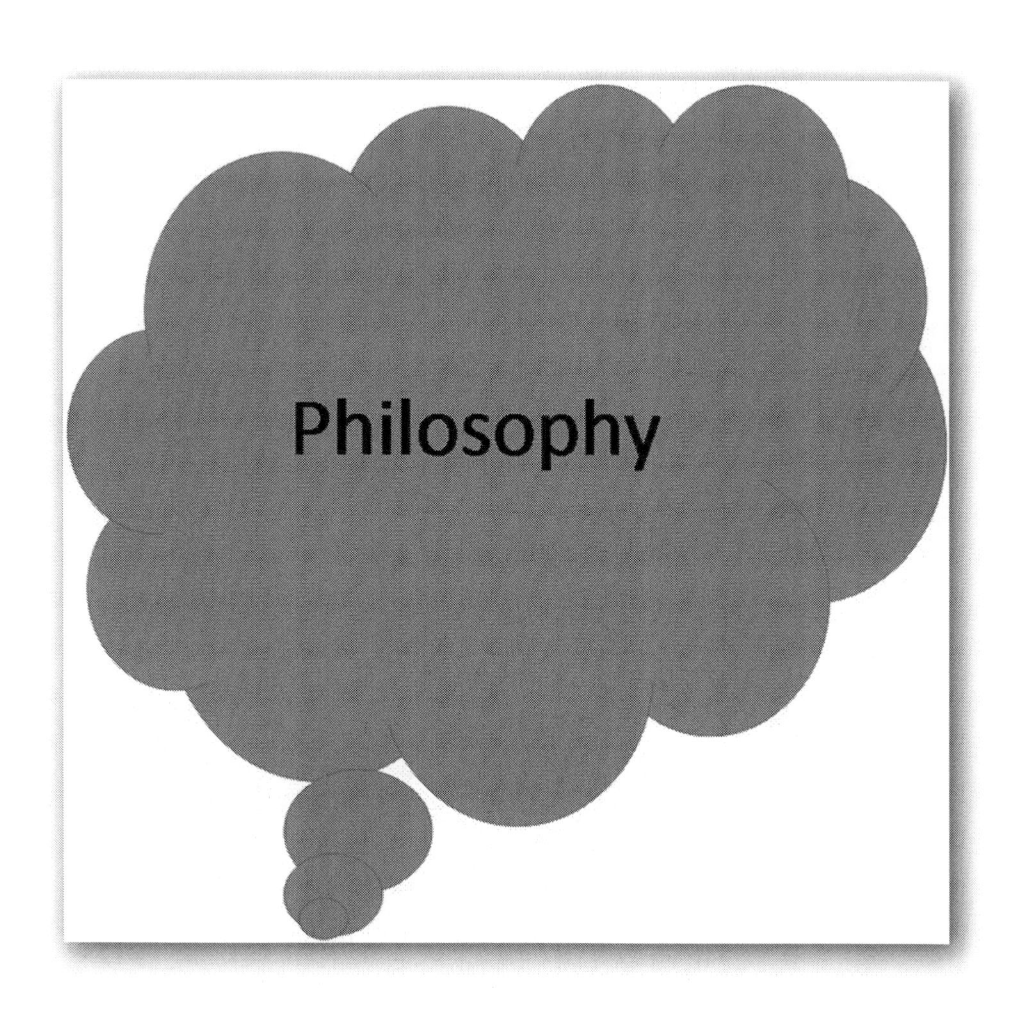
Philosophy

Philosophy

To Snooze or Not to Snooze?

I am a snoozer. My husband is not. He simply cannot understand my whole waking up in the morning system. He doesn't really have a system, so, well, I think I win. Of course, I have a job I have to get up for and he doesn't, so maybe he wins after all.

My alarm clock is broken. I mean, it will ring when the numbers on the 'alarm' setting match the numbers on the 'time' setting, but it can't keep track of time any better than a preschooler in time-out can. It runs fast, but not consistently fast. The time on its face is some random time ahead of the real time, although usually within the hour. Usually. Not always.

This drives my husband bonkers, even though from where he lays his head at night he can't see the thing, and he has a clock right next to his head that tells the correct time. I love it this way. If I lie in bed in the morning and know I have exactly X number of minutes until I am late, you can guarantee I won't get up until X + several minutes have gone by, under the theory that I can just take a quick shower and maybe do my makeup at work. However, if I have no idea if I am already late, I have some incentive to get up because I really really hate being late. So setting a 'normal' clock ahead wouldn't work because I would know how many minutes to add.

I also like to snooze the alarm, another thing that irritates my beloved. His argument is that it isn't like you get any actual sleep in the nine minutes between cathedral bells (another reason I like my alarm clock) and won't be any more rested after three or four snoozes.

His argument, I believe, shows a fundamental lack of understanding of how my brain operates. I don't know about you, but I don't have an on and off switch. I'm not either 'awake' or 'asleep.' There are transition periods. In fact, I'm pretty sure that if you put your ear close to my head during the 27 minutes of snooze time, you would hear some electrical crackling noise as the synapses fire up and prepare for the day's onslaught of input. I need time to reflect on my dream while I am halfway asleep and the thing still makes a modicum of sense. I need time to steel my nerves for whatever fresh hell the day is going to bring me.

My husband and my son are like robots, in my opinion. They power on and power off. There is nothing gradual about it. My son is either sleeping or he is awake. He is never sleepy, out of it, daydreaming, lost in thought, or in la la land. When he was small, the only way we could get him to fall asleep was to get him to stop talking. The minute he did, he would conk out.

My daughter and I need some time in an in-between state. I have an elaborate bed time ritual, and if one step is missed, or even done out of order, the whole process seems out of whack and might not even work at all. I have to have a glass of milk. I have to wash my face, floss, and brush. In that order. I have to read at least ten pages of fiction. You cannot talk to me. Not even to say goodnight, or I have to start at a certain point all over again. I have to read on my left side, then turn over on my stomach, think for a while, and then turn to my right. I hug my bear, named Whip (don't ask), to my chest. This is important to my health and well being. I don't know why. I don't care why. I simply know it works.

A few days ago, my husband reset my clock to reflect the actual time. He told me he was doing this. I suppose I could have stopped him, but I didn't. Truly, I have no idea now what time I should set my alarm for in order to get up on time. I've been late for every single thing that has happened in the morning since. It is hard for me to wrap my dream-drunk morning brain around looking at the clock and accepting that the number on it is for real.

Reality. It shouldn't be faced before coffee.

The Inherent Value of Suffering

Recently, my family took a road trip to visit my parents in Ft. Myers, Florida. We've taken this trip many times. It is about six hundred miles, door to door, mostly on long, boring stretches of I-75, with not much to look at but billboards offering vasectomies, strippers, religious salvation, and outlet malls, not necessarily in that order. There are plenty of construction notices. There are miles and miles of orange cones and barrels, and even some bits of torn up roadway and construction equipment, but precious little actual constructing going on.

We usually take this route during spring break, along with most of the eastern seaboard, and many people to the west of the Mississippi. My son, bored enough to resort to old school car games, managed to see license plates from 38 out of the 50 states, as well as two Provinces in Canada. There is a lot of traffic. Often, it is stop and go. More stop than go.

It has the potential to be a disaster. It is a dry, wooden tinderbox in a lightning storm.

My kids complain. There is plenty to complain about. They're tired. They're physically uncomfortable. They have to go to the bathroom. They're hungry. They're bored. They complain despite access to iPods and a built in DVD player and arts & crafts supplies and books and filtered air flowing precisely the chosen temperature. Inevitably, my husband and I feel compelled to tell them to quit it because (cue wavery old-person voice and shaking fist) back in my day we had no air conditioning and sat without seat belts on vinyl upholstery that made the back of your thighs stick, with the silver metal buckles and other car-related hardware that reached temperatures hot enough to melt rock branding your knees and elbows, with the AM-only radio blaring something staticky only an old person could possibly find entertaining, and oh by the way the windows were all the way rolled up and my parents smoked like chimneys so that the air was thick and hazy. Quitcher bellyaching with your cushy individualized captain's chair, SpongeBob on demand, and earbuds spitting out whatever song you choose in perfect privacy.

We say this in a condescending way, like there is some inherent value in suffering that our pampered children are never going to benefit from. You will never be as good as I am, goes the subtext, because you are soft and squishy and don't know how to tolerate real discomfort.

Naturally, they resent this.

It is as useful a discourse as telling them they should eat their yummy Brussels sprouts because there are children starving in China. It doesn't make the Brussels sprouts taste any more like chocolate ice cream.

Often, with a little funky raincloud of irritation over my head, I bemoan the fate of humanity. We are raising the least tough generation to date. These kids have no idea how to do without. They get twitchy and anxious at the first sign of a lack of Wi-Fi. They don't know what it is like to wait all year for the Wizard of Oz to come on television because if you didn't see it that night you weren't going to see it until the next year.

Then it finally dawned on me. So what? Exactly when are they going to have to sit in an uncomfortable, smoky car without air conditioning, or even have to wait to see a movie or television show they feel like watching? They don't even have to watch commercials if they don't want to, except if they are in a hotel room, and then only if the Wi-Fi isn't working. The ability to put up with what I put up with is about as useful to them as the ability to fire a musket. Sure, it is *possible* they might have to do such a thing, but it is entirely unlikely.

I then remembered camp. My kids go to Camp Chatuga every year, and have since before they can remember that they didn't. This will be my son's 6th year, and my daughter's 5th. While there, they don't have air conditioning, Wi-Fi or any other electronics, and they sleep in rickety bunks with thin, crinkly mattresses. And they love every second of it. Fifty years from now, if you mention Camp Chatuga to them, I am certain they will get the same misty look in their eye that they get now. To them, that gnat-filled place is paradise. They don't think of the creature comforts that they lack, they think of the gorgeous scenery, campfires, swimming, games, friends, and private jokes.

I felt better. Complaining in the back seat while on an interminable car trip is as American as apple pie, baseball, and Netflix. I'm proud to be able to provide for my children as many things as I can, and proud that they also know other ways to have fun and enjoy themselves. And I'll tell you this – those earphones that allow them to watch whatever ridiculous movie they want in the back seat while blocking out whatever it is that my husband and I are saying to each other? Priceless.

Creature Comforts

When I was a little girl, I loved *The Little House on the Prairie.* Both the book series, which I read about nine million times (though mostly the first two books), and the TV series, which came out when I was exactly the target age for it. Melissa Gilbert, the actress who played Laura Ingalls, and I are roughly the same age. I wasn't much interested in Laura's crush on Almanzo Wilder. I was more interested in how she could possibly survive without the things I had.

I was the kind of dreamy kid who could spend hours in the back yard all by myself playing 'pretend' and most likely talking to myself out loud. One of my favorite games was imagining what would happen if I could somehow bring Laura into my time and show her around. I pointed up in the sky and showed her airplanes and explained how normal it was for people to strap themselves into a giant metal tube and fly across the country. I let her sit on the vinyl seats in the back of the station wagon and be amazed that we didn't need any horses and could roll down the windows with a crank. She was impressed – she thought I was the luckiest girl in the world for living in such modern times.

I was afraid she wouldn't like me, though. Laura was a much better, purer person than I was. I remember one time she thought about slapping her sister, Mary, and felt horrible about even having the thought. Given the number of times I might have actually hit my sister in the years I only had only one digit in my age, I knew she'd think I was just mean and heartless. I thought about Laura when I was mad because I didn't get to drink out of my favorite cup – I remembered the scene where she and her sister Mary get their OWN tin cup to SHARE and they were excited about it. Whoa. It kinda put my fights over the collector's glass with Ronald McDonald on it (painted with lead paint, no doubt) in perspective.

I thought about her today. My husband is now on day ten of his "replacing the steps to the deck" project. There are four steps. They have been out of commission for months. I thought of Laura's Pa cutting down trees and hauling them over to the homestead site without the benefit of a combustion engine to build their Little House on the Prairie. I think it took Charles Ingalls less time to build an entire house, albeit a tiny, drafty one, than it has taken Mike to rebuild four stairs. And Charles didn't have Home Depot or Lowes. Or Ace Hardware. Or even Sears. For that matter, he had to shoot dinner in between ax strokes and rigging hand-carved pulleys to get the logs high enough to make a roof.

What soft people we have become. My kids get twitchy when they don't have access to Wi-Fi. Even if I managed to kill a wabbit, I wouldn't know exactly what to do in order to turn it into food. I'm irritated at the moment because my dishwasher is broken, and I have to wash my dishes BY HAND with the hot and cold running water that just comes out of my spigot on demand. My husband, who is a fairly competent carpenter and handyman (not to be confused with an efficient one), needs (or so he claims) about four different power drills and three chainsaws, and an entire garage full of other tools. All this so he can spend two weeks replacing four plain, unfinished wooden steps. We'd die from exposure if he had to build us a warm house before winter set in while I was hand sewing clothes and knitting socks from wool I got directly from the neighbor's sheep and hauling up water from a creek three-quarters of a mile away one gallon at a time.

My daughter in particular, though she loves dystopian fiction where people survive all kinds of poverty, deprivation, and people-trying-to-kill-them, would not likely survive the first five minutes if she went to visit Laura Ingalls in her time. My daughter's mind would be thinking all of the necessities of life that she would never get on the prairie. Wi-fi, Netflix, and Starbucks would be running through her mind faster than she could actually run. Likely, she would die of grief.

She's not alone. We live in a time where independent children are the ones who pour processed bowls of cereal out of a box for themselves and then leave the bowl in the sink for the dish fairy to contend with later.

And I'll tell you this – thank goodness for that. There is no shame in poverty or deprivation, but there is no essential virtue in it either. I unapologetically love my creature comforts. I'm sorry that everyone doesn't have them, but that doesn't make me want to give them up. I have great affection for my central heating and my air conditioning and my running water and my soft supportive bed made out of synthetic fibers. I like not having any idea what part of a cow the 'sirloin' is. I revel in the delusion that butter is naturally formed into quarter pound sticks wrapped in waxed paper without effort on anyone's part.

Yup. Laura can come visit me. But I'm not going to visit her.

You Can't Always Get What You Want

Theoretically, I have standards. First world, developed nation standards. Upper middle class standards beyond that, even. Not just clean water and delicious, plentiful food, and no military juntas at the door, but beautiful, peaceful living space with useless, but pretty, tasteful décor. I have fantasies of having the kind of house that makes people walk in and gasp audibly with wonder. I guess they do gasp audibly, and probably in wonder, but it is more like, "GASP! I wonder how a grown, educated woman with a decent job and able-bodied family members can survive in such complete chaos."

I don't have a knack for objects. I have a collection of beautiful crystal bowls and vases, most of which I received as wedding presents back when we partied like it was 1999 because it was in fact 1999. I have a mantelpiece over a marble fireplace, and halogen lights that point in that direction. Theoretically, that part of the house should gleam in gorgeous lead crystal radiant rainbow glory. However, due to a shortage of walls in our 'open floor plan' house, my non-negotiable piano is parked in front of the fireplace, and, in addition to the inartfully placed crystal on the mantle there are dunes of dust and random toys and remote controls and cups and half-completed art projects that make it look more like a shelf in a second rate thrift shop.

I'd like to think I have the equipment to make a nice arrangement. Someone else could make the same objects look beautiful. My friend Sheri, for example, has a knack for objects. I'd let Sheri tackle my house, but I'm embarrassed to let her come over. She decorated the lobby in my office, and she bought this completely non-descript silver swirly decorative object that made me initially think "what the....?" She placed it Just So on the table, and suddenly the whole room was pulled together. If she had somehow produced a fully grown elephant out of her purse I wouldn't have been more impressed.

I don't have that skill. I admire that skill.

Recently, I went to a dinner at the home of a very gracious, kind, generous woman who was hosting a potluck dinner for a group to which I belong. I stepped into her foyer. (Technically, I have a foyer. There is a square of floor that isn't part of any other room in the entry way of my house. It has a coat rack and a book shelf, and about seven thousand scarves and book bags strewn about.) It was instantly clear that I was outclassed by a mile. Photographs with matching frames hung on the wall. Collections of like objects were arranged in a pleasing way. I was on the early side, and the first to arrive. My hostess mentioned that she had just finished setting up and she was already exhausted. She asked me if I entertained often.

I was unsure how to respond. The thought that flew into my brain was, "No. Not by a long shot. I'm too embarrassed to let other 11 year olds in my home, much less a collection of judgey grownups." Instead, I said, "Not often. My kids are in charge. Ha ha!"

I had driven a ways to get to her house, and I needed to use the rest room. She pointed me in the right direction. I shut the door, and did a basic scan of the room to make sure that there was toilet paper, soap, and a towel, necessities that you can't take for granted in my house. Not only was there toilet paper, soap, and several towels, but the toilet paper had been tied into a little rose.

The rose was adorable. For someone who knew what they were doing, it couldn't have taken more than 45 seconds to do. The rose depressed the bejeebers out of me. I don't even stay at hotels that have such fancy toilet paper. I feel like I'm living large in a nice hotel when the TP has been folded into a point. In my own home, I'm merely happy when something vaguely absorbent and biodegradable is within arm's reach. On the few occasions when I do have guests, the last few moments before they arrive are spent kicking the last few items of detritus underneath the sofa for easy, out of the way storage, and figuring there will be enough feet on the floor that no one will notice I didn't have time to mop. Never in a thousand years would I consider making the toilet paper look pretty.

I wasn't sure what to do with the rose, besides get photographic evidence. I didn't want to use it for its intended purpose, so I carefully ripped it off and replaced it after I got what I needed. I didn't need to go hunting for corn cobs or the Sears catalogue, so all was good.

A Rolling Stone song. That's what it all boils down to, isn't it? I got what I needed. Toilet paper roses and toilet paper wads flush the same way and serve the same purpose. You can't always get what you want. But, at least in my middle class existence, I always get what I need.

Desire

I'm not saying that I don't like having a high capacity washer and dryer in my house. Don't think for a second that I'd prefer to go down to the creek with a paddle and a bar of lye soap I made myself to beat my clothes against a rock and then wring them out by hand and hang them on a line and pray that it doesn't rain and/or that a flock of geese doesn't travel overhead. Nope, I am happy to be able to stick my clothes in a machine, walk away, stick them in another machine, walk away again, and then spend ten minutes folding them.

But.

But, because it is so easy, there isn't any excuse for not doing it. Back in the day I would only be expected to own one or two dresses, and one or both of them would usually be some variation on dirty because washing was such an ordeal. Our standards have changed along with the inventions that make standards possible. Because I have a vacuum cleaner, there shouldn't be crunchy things on my carpet. Because I have bubbles that will scrub for me, my bathroom should be sparkly clean and smell vaguely like cleaning products at all times. And because all these things are done by machine and technology, I should also be able to hold down a job, be active in the PTO, help with the homework, work on the weekends to raise money for the Band Boosters, and stay caught up on politics, sports, and the latest television shows and novels.

I'm also not saying that I want to go back to the Victorian era, when I wouldn't have been able to vote or show my ankles in public. But. I would kind of like those lowered expectations. Back in the day, you were only expected to do one thing. If I were an upper-middle class woman in 1890, I would have a laundress to do the laundry, a governess/nanny to deal with the children, a cook to deal with feeding my family, and a maid to keep the house clean. My time would be spent embroidering, practicing the piano, and engaging in charitable works.

I want to know how, in the scant 125 years since then, things have changed so much. Largely for the better – I could not have been a lawyer then, certainly not a judge, and I know for certain that I would have died during the birth of my son.

It's just that lately, the whole concept of possibility seems burdensome. If it is possible, then I should try to do it or get it or achieve it. Otherwise I'm lazy, or squandering my potential, right? That said, wasn't it Buddha who said that desire is the root of all suffering? If things don't exist, they can't be desired. If you desire something you can't get or have or achieve, then you are disappointed. If you don't want, you aren't disappointed.

Sometimes, when I am driving from point A to point B, I will see a little house in the middle of not much of anywhere. Sometimes I think, "why would anyone live here?" The house will be neat and tidy, but not especially luxurious, and there aren't too many amenities within easy driving distance. Going to the movies or a concert would be a road trip. Buying anything you can't find in the Piggly Wiggly would be an ordeal. There aren't museums or ball fields or town greens with live music. There aren't any restaurants that serve any food that might use the word "fusion" as a descriptor.

Other times, when I look at those little houses, I am jealous of the people who live there. I imagine the house being paid for, or the mortgage payment being negligible. I imagine the residents tending a small vegetable garden. Tomatoes in the summer, beans in the fall, winter squash. I imagine them drinking coffee every morning on the front porch watching the world wake up. Dinner is set in a crock pot. Bread is set to rise. Maybe I'll paint today. Or build some more bookshelves for the basement. Or learn to change the oil in my own car. I could bake cupcakes for the bake sale.

There's nothing wrong with a small life. In fact, there's a lot right about it. If you've got food, clothing, shelter, and relative health, everything else is window dressing. I mean, who cares how many people buy my books. The joy was in the writing: the art of creation, no? Ok, no. I care how many books are sold. You should immediately buy many copies of this book to give to your friends for all gift giving occasions, as well as copies of my other two books, which I will shamelessly plug here[2]. My spirit is big enough to want to want less, but not big enough to give up personal ambition and desire. I desire to desire less, but I don't desire less, so I suffer because of my desire not to desire.

Meditate on that.

2 They are called "Mismatched Shoes and Upside Down Pizza" and "The Armadillo, the Pickaxe, and the Laundry Basket" and they are, if I do say so myself, masterpieces. Or at least I desire for them to be called such.

Mom Jeans

I've had a longstanding rule at my lake house. The house, located in the muddy armpit of Lake Oconee, is designed to be an oasis. Nothing stressful is supposed to happen there. We have no television access, so you can't watch the news to find out who was brutally murdered or who was maimed in a tragic accident. We have no internet access, so your cousin's Facebook posts about whatever political topic makes your hair stand on end are invisible to you. Only if you stand the right way in a certain place and wear an aluminum foil hat do you even get cell phone reception.

On top of all that, I have a very strict "no pants and no restrictive undergarments" rule. This is not to say that we run around unclothed. At all times, all the parts that you'd like to see covered up are, in fact, covered up. Rather, this rule means that in the summer you should be wearing a bathing suit or pajamas or, if you absolutely must, shorts with an elastic waistband. Nothing should poke you, or restrict you, or leave red lines on your skin from where you've been squeezed for several hours. The point of this rule is that you should be comfortable. This is a hedonistic place: if it doesn't make you happy, we don't want it here. Uncomfortable clothes make you crabby. Crabby is the opposite of happy.

I'm lucky. I can take an actual photograph of my happy place, and I own the deed to the land it sits on. Lucky me.

So, given all that I have and what I know, you'd think that sometime before my forty-fifth year on the planet before I realized the secret to happiness is not contained in a rickety house bordered by a chocolate milk brown lake. You can have this kind of happiness anywhere. The key to it all? The secret that I could sell for a fortune, that I'm giving you right here, right now, for free?

It is this: Pants that fit, and shoes that are shaped like feet.

That's it. It's that simple. It's why men seem happier than women most of the time – their pants are designed to fit. Their shoes are wider in the front and don't shift the center of balance. Our pants are designed to look good, our shoes are designed to look cute, to lengthen our legs and engage our calf muscles. Comfort is usually somewhere around 27th or 28th on the list of the priorities.

Recently, I discovered that there are a number of brands of jeans (none, sadly, of the discount variety) that are designed for, well, grown-ups. My favorite, as much for the clever name as the fit, is a brand called "Not Your Daughter's Jeans." Isn't that brilliant? Because the truth is that even though I weigh roughly the same as I did in the early 90's, my shape is only vaguely related to my shape back then. (I am still, thank goodness, taller than I am wide, and my head is still on top of my neck. Beyond that, it's all different.) Just like a 100 pound lead weight and a 100 pound sack of feathers aren't going to be anywhere close to the same size or shape, I'm neither the size nor shape than I was at 18. I'm curvier now. Gravity has made me bottom heavy, and things droop that didn't used to.

My body has been through a number of transformations. I've been thin in my lifetime. I've been squishy, and I've been buff. I've had entire human beings crammed in the fetal position (ha ha) in my belly. There is no way that even if we weighed the same that my daughter and I could be shaped the same, or wanting to highlight the body parts.

I *like* Mom jeans. I like not having to worry about my pants slipping down like a plumber's. I like a little roominess in the back. The last thing on this planet I want is a hard denim seam sneaking its way into the seam God gave me. I like fabric that doesn't try to fight me when I lean over. I like not feeling the irresistible urge to say "oof" every time I have to bend something more than 90 degrees. I appreciate a pair of pants that can accommodate a lunch buffet or the occasional bloating that occurs when you accidentally eat an entire jar of pickles.

So who's with me? Let us over forties dress like over forties, not millenials. Let us be happy because we can take a whole breath in without worrying about a button popping. No matter what I do I can't fight the fact that I was born in the pre-Watergate Nixon era. I'm not going to fool anyone by wearing low rise skinny jeans with an intentional rip in the knee.

You can have your fashions. I am *not* wearing my daughter's jeans.

If I Had a Jillion Dollars

I would make a fabulous rich person. I don't mean merely a person with a lot of money, I mean one of those ridiculously rich people who are worth so much that it isn't worth their time to stoop to pick up a twenty dollar bill.

Hear me out – I'm not saying the world *needs* people with that kind of scratch, I'm just saying that if the world *has* to have those kinds of people, I think I should be one of them. I am worthy, and want to plead my case.

Don't get me wrong: I would build my dream house, complete with a library with one of those rolling ladder things and big leather armchairs and ottomans, a music room with grand piano and kickin' sound system, a home theater, and a gym complete with on-staff trainer and masseuse. But that's just for ME. And it would employ quite a few contractors and sub-contractors and architects and decorators and chauffeurs and masseuses. I would personally reduce the unemployment rate.

I would stimulate the economy by buying a lot of nice gifts for those people who have been nice to me. Nice gifts. Not the kind you plaster on a fake grin for and then stick in a closet until you figure out who else you can pawn it off on. I would even buy some gifts for some people who haven't been nice to me, just to show that I am a kind and benevolent person who is able to forgive, even if I never ever ever will forget. (Forgiving is healthy. Forgetting is for fools.) I would buy all of these gifts from local merchants and buy as many handmade, unique items as I could to support local artists and to reward creativity.

I would also do good works. I would give an endowment to the Boys & Girls Club in Monroe so they would never have to scramble for money and so they could pay the staff handsomely to get the best of the best.

I would make sure that my synagogue stayed financially sound.

I would start a philanthropy called "The Kickstart Foundation" which would offer no-strings-attached micro-loans to people who just need a kickstart in order to get started. You know. Victims of domestic violence. Foster children who have just graduated from the system. The working poor with whopping medical bills. Deserving people who just need a hand.

I would open a book store that probably wouldn't be self-supporting, but which would provide a great service. I would only feature books that are written well, which would knock out a lot of bestsellers. I would highlight struggling, talented indie authors. It would be decorated with paintings and other artwork from undiscovered artists, all for sale. I would only employ people who get excited by questions like, "What should I read next?" Underneath each book on the shelf would be a little card with a note from someone who works at my store (or me) saying what we liked about it. If no one has read it, and/or if no one likes it, it doesn't get sold.

Naturally, there would be coffee sold there at reasonable prices. There should be coffee everywhere. Coffee makes everything better. I would start a campaign to make it the national beverage.

I would give money to politicians that I support (assuming I could actually find one worth supporting) anonymously to avoid the buying and selling of offices or even the appearance of it.

I would make sure my children were comfortable, but not too comfortable. The best schools, the best opportunities, but not enough in their trust funds to live off of for a lifetime, unless they live frugally. Of course, given my daughter's current love of Ramen Noodles, she could probably pull it off. All she wants right now is Ramen Noodles and Netflix. I'm pretty sure she would live in a box so long as she had Ramen Noodles and Netflix and an oversized hoodie.

I would somehow figure out a way to buy coolness for band geeks everywhere.

In conclusion, I'd be a great jillionaire. Don't you think? Don't you want me to be fabulously wealthy so I can make all this a reality? I just have to figure out how to get that way. Simply being deserving of it is not making it happen. Any ideas? I mean, aside from buying jillions of copies of this book and giving it to everyone you know.

Hey. That would work. Make it so, friends.

PUHHHHHHH-din

I love the way my friend Diane says the word "pudding." She says "PUHHHHHHHHH-din," with the "puh" drawn out for three whole seconds and the "din" just a little flip of the back of the throat, almost not even there. I ate some pudding today, and I asked her to say the word before I ate it. She obliged. And then told me there was really no other way to say it.

"For you," I said. "But you speak southern. Imagine if I said 'For Thanksgiving we had turkey and carrots and mashed potatoes and broccoli and PUHHHHHHHHHdin.' It would sound ridiculous."

She said, "I would never say that. I'd say, 'We had turkey an' dressin' and PUHHHHHHdin for dessert.'"

Which lead to a "dressing" vs. "stuffing" conversation. I say stuffing, because you stuff the stuff *inside* the turkey. Dressing would imply that it went on *top* of the turkey, which it doesn't. Still, you can't argue with words your Mama taught you.

I go to the movies. Diane goes to the THEEayter.

I don't really speak with any accent. My upbringing was in three different states in the south and southwest in the learning to speak years, and the north during the formative years, and then college and law school at schools with large Yankee populations in the south, all the while under the direct influence of my stereotypical Yankee parents. I sort of speak television neutral, but I may get more Southern or Yankee depending upon who I am talking to. When I'm mad, I'm more Yankee. When I'm trying to get what I want, I'm more Southern. Until I get mad.

I LOVE regional accents. I wish I had one for real.

Diane, who starts to get itchy when she gets more than 15 miles from home, is one of my favorite accented people, and one of my favorite games is comparing how we say things. She thinks "Merry, marry, and Mary" are all pronounced identically. I think they are three different words. Likewise, she says "pin" and "pen" the same (peeeeeyun). And "still" and "steel." Often, I have to ask her to clarify.

It is fun to watch Diane and my Mom have a conversation. Between my mother's thick Brooklynese (and increasing deafness) and Diane's drawl it is rather entertaining. I find myself switching accents like languages and translating.

My Mom, unlike Diane, says her g's but will often drop her r's. Never fear – there is a law of conservation of r's. For every "r" that falls off of "water" (wah-tuh) it is added to "banana" (buhNAHnner.) Once, when I was in college, I had been sick, and told my mother that my cough was better. "What?" she said. I repeated myself. She repeated her what. Then I realized the problem. I said, "My CAWF is bettah!" and she said, "Oh, good."

So nice. So nice to be understood by those we love.

I Ate Some Pie

It's been a while since I wrote about how much I like food, but I hope that does not make you think for a second that I have quit eating for the sheer pleasure of it.

I'm having a bad day. I mean, not in the way that people in Prisoner of War camps have bad days, or schizophrenic homeless people in cold weather have bad days, but I'm having a bad day in my upper middle class way. It isn't only the person who is suffering the most in this world who is entitled to wallow in the black swirl of a pity party from time to time. The fact that your problem is worse than mine doesn't make mine any less painful to me.

After a lunch consisting of questionably old beef stew (still tasty – is there anything wrong with preferring my own cooking to just about anyone else's?) I was still feeling dissatisfied. Disobedient children, clients who don't pay my bills or appreciate my services, Pacific northwest persistent rain in what is supposed to be the sunny south, sick loved ones, and a general feeling of exhaustion all conspired to make me feel, in a word, yucky.

It's hard to be funny when you feel yucky. I pride myself on being funny. I need to make the yucky go away.

So I got in my car and drove across the street to McDonald's and got me some apple pies. I distributed them, Santa like, to the people in my office from their paper sack, spreading fried-apple flavored sunshine in my wake.

I get it. Going for a brisk walk is probably healthier than eating fast food pie, and has longer lasting effects in beating off depression and anxiety. But what if one of the reasons why I am anxious is because I have 4935 unread emails in my Inbox? I can whittle that number down while eating pie. I can't do anything during a brisk walk but briskly walk. I can bury my nose in a cup of French roast coffee while reading case law, I can eat a gorgeous pile of Pasta Primavera while talking to my husband about his day, and I can eat a dish of ice cream while trying to figure out how to simplify radicals to help my 8th grader do his math homework.

Of course, food is better when you don't multi-task it. I would just as soon not even see or hear anything when I put a piece of something wonderful and complex in my mouth. Sometimes I'll even close my eyes. The salt on the side of my tongue, the sweet in the back, the savory dead center...it's like listening to perfect harmony in music.

Pie never disappoints. People are inherently unreliable, even the ones you love, and even when they don't mean to be. There is no one on this Earth who lives or should live solely for the purpose of attending to my every desire at the moment that I desire it. People have their own needs, their own agendas, and look out for their own number ones. But not pie. Pie just sits there. Nobody needs pie. Pie isn't a food group recognized by any credible dietary agency, though maybe it should be. Pie is a luxury. Pie is a sign that you have enough, and want just a little more. Pie waits to be eaten. It wants to be eaten. Its sole purpose, its *raison d'etre,* is to give pleasure to whomever decides to eat it whenever they decide to eat it. There's no such thing as punishment pie[3]. Pie is a reward. And the fact that I got through today without committing any felonies or screeching like a crazy person at everyone and everything that irritated me means I deserve a reward.

Yup, that was me. I ate some pie. And I'm not ashamed.

---

3 Ok, except maybe meat pies, which shouldn't be called pies, and will forever in my mind be associated with Mrs. Lovett's pie shop, and my lack of desire to "try the priest." (Please, someone get that joke.) Or mincemeat pies, which don't have meat in them, but might actually be pie. Honestly, I've never had one because it makes me suspicious.

There's No Place Like Home

One day in the not too distant future, when I have more than three recreational hours in a row, I would like to travel the world. I want to go to Italy and see the art that virtually litters every street corner. I want to dive the Great Barrier Reef in Australia. I want to take a tour of the wine country in northern California, and drink champagne in the actual Champagne region of France. I want to go to Ireland and Scotland and see London and Paris and Tokyo and Hawaii and Costa Rica and many other places I've read about in books and seen on television. I'd like to take a road trip around America in search of the World's Greatest Burger and stop at all the tacky tourist traps like the world's largest ball of twine.

I know from the few trips I took pre-children that there are some things that you simply cannot appreciate unless you are there. A picture of a thousands of years old Roman aqueduct or biblical-era fort is one thing. To touch it is another. A picture of a small dot of a person standing atop Hoover Dam makes you realize it is big: Standing next to it is an entirely different scale of things.

But I have a problem. The problem is that I am a real homebody. It is a big deal to get me out of my house for a social occasion. Packing things up and going somewhere unfamiliar? Not my favorite.

This is why all my vacation money goes into paying for my lake house. I can "get away from it all" in a place where my drawers are already in the drawers, and I know exactly where the mugs and coffee are kept.

It is really stupid how I feel about this, and I fear my children's horizons will be narrower than they should be because I like being in familiar surroundings. It is pathological. I mean, take how I felt a few weeks ago. I'd been visiting my parents in Ft. Myers, Florida. Although that isn't the town and theirs isn't the house I grew up in, my folks have lived in this house for about ten years now, and some of the furniture and dishes are the same as I remember from childhood. In fact, I noticed that my Dad has had the same flip-flops I remember from the early 70s. This is about as familiar as a place that isn't mine is going to get. I know exactly where everything is and what to bring (and not bring) and what I am and am not allowed to do. I don't have to worry about fitting in to the local culture. This is the local culture that raised me.

And yet. In my house, there are only three places I would put my phone. None of those three places are here, so I am constantly looking for it. I took my driver's license, a credit card, and a twenty dollar bill out of my wallet and stuck it in my pocket so I wouldn't have to bring my purse when we went out. I spent two days after that forgetting to put them back in my wallet, and freaking out every time I went to pay for something. I can't do my bedtime routine. I wake up every morning and spend the first ten seconds trying to figure out where I am. I can't keep track of my bath towel. I forgot a razor, and so I'm desperately trying to tan my legs so as to camouflage the stubble.

I'm a creature of habit. In my natural habitat, I'm a bit of an absent-minded professor. I can still remember the home phone of my best friend when I was nine. I can recall enough useless information on command that I was a real live contestant on Jeopardy! and made a pretty good showing at it[4]. I am good with academic recall. That said, I rarely remember to bring the lunch I made and set on the counter. I can't keep track of my keys or sunglasses or reading glasses. And so, over the years, I have developed a great arsenal of compensating behaviors. I know exactly where my checkbook is and where all the bills to be paid are, because there is only one place I would put them. My keys are only in one place. I keep a pair of reading glasses in each place I am likely to need them. (In my purse, on my desk at work, next to my bed, next to

4 Don't believe me? I triple-dog dare you to Google "Lori Duff Jeopardy" and see what you come up with.

the place where I do the most crossword puzzles, and next to the La-Z-Boy in the living room.)

I can't do that when I'm not at home. Every single time I have gone on a trip I have had to buy a pair of sunglasses at a gas station or a dollar store because I can't find (or forgot to bring) the pair I bought the last time I went out of town. My keys, my phone, my laptop, and my purse are always missing. I never get the right number of shirts/pants/socks in my suitcase. I feel out of sorts. My digestive system doesn't do what it is supposed to do. I want to go home. I don't want to leave where I am, but I want to go home. I'll miss my parents the second I leave, but that doesn't stop me from wanting to sleep in my own bed.

Dadblast it, you know what I forgot to pack? My ruby slippers. Oz is a great place to visit and all, but truly, there is no place like home.

A Room of My Own

I've been married now for 3,129.285 years. So it seems. Things that happened before I got married seem somewhat unreal, almost like they are memories of a movie I once saw rather than things that actually happened to me.

So, needless to say, the honeymoon stage is over. Way over. My husband and I have lived in the same house for so long that it is impossible to keep up pretense. He knows the raw me, the one that has morning breath that could peel paint, the one that is snippy and snappy after a long day at work, and the one that hates wearing makeup and tailored clothing. He's seen me be sick, he's been there when I gave birth, and he's seen my actual reactions to things that in public I've been rather stoic about.

All of which is a long introduction to say that once the face you put on for the public, the polite one, the shiny one goes away, it ain't ever coming back.

I work, at the moment, three jobs. My husband earned his retirement after thirty years of public safety (Police, Fire, AND *EMS*) with DeKalb County and stays at home and collects a pension. As a result, I tend to get a little bit more exhausted by the end of the day than he does, and just like our days start at different times, they end at different times as well. I have a great deal of trouble staying up past 11, and I rarely even try. My husband is a night owl. He kicks it into high gear somewhere around midnight, banging things around and digging through plastic bags to find what he needs. I like things neat and organized. My husband's organizational method can best be described as "one giant pile of random things strategically placed for maximum trippage in the middle of the night."

And so, when my daughter packed up her stuff and left us to go to camp this summer for three weeks, I took my book and my reading glasses and my alarm clock and my teddy bear and took a little staycation and moved into her room. It seemed like a big deal, like a comment on something bigger than it was. But really? I just want to sleep in the dark and in the quiet and in a neat and organized environment. (Note: my daughter's room is not, as a general rule, neat and organized. It usually looks like the police have just finished executing a search warrant at the home of a suspected drug lord. But it is neat and organized now that there is no one but me to interfere with the contents.) The first night, I was afraid that I would be nervous and uncomfortable and would stare at the ceiling all night worrying.

Nope. I passed out instantly and didn't wake up until the alarm rang. That, folks, is a miracle for me.

I also realized that her mattress, a memory foam one, is seriously comfortable.

I've enjoyed having my own personal space. I found myself jealous of my kids who have their own space. (Two of their own spaces, if you count their rooms at the lake house.) I mean, how come they are entitled to privacy and their own corner(s) of the world, and I pay the mortgage(s), and I have to share mine? In what universe does that make sense?

Our house is relatively small, only three bedrooms, so there isn't anywhere for me to claim as my own. This experience, though, makes me want to sell my house and buy a bigger one just so I can have my own room. I haven't had my own room since, well, let's just say that if I had a baby the last time I had my own room, that baby would be going off to college in a few weeks.

The other day my husband said to me, "I've missed having you in the bed, but I don't really miss your snoring."

I nodded gravely. "I miss you, too," I said. "But I don't miss you rattling your 50,000 baby food jars filled with assorted screws and nuts and bolts around at midnight after turning on the lights to find them."

I'm not sure what I'm going to do when my daughter returns from camp. If both of my children were the same gender I'd make them share a room.

But they're not. My son goes to college in only five short years, and there will be tons of camps and sleepovers outside the house between now and then to give me some respite. I've waited this long. I guess I can wait a little bit longer.

In the meantime, a girl can dream. Assuming she can get to sleep, that is.

The Bill of Parents' Rights

First Amendment: Free Speech

The fact that you have given birth to a child, adopted a child, or in some other way claimed a young 'un for your own in no way shape or form limits your right to free speech. If you spill the pink drink in the car, especially if it splashes back on your white pants, you are entitled to free use of any words in your vocabulary, even the ones that make you put a quarter in the swear jar.

Second Amendment: Right To Bear Arms

A well regulated militia, indeed, is what is required to maintain order when your children come home from tying on the cotton candy, Coke, and frosting at a birthday party. Bear arms, wooden spoons, time out chairs, or whatever is necessary to keep footprints off your ceiling. Also, don't forget your "bear arms" for giving (and getting) bear hugs whenever necessary.

Third Amendment: No Soldier Shall Be Quartered Without The Homeowner's Permission

That kid from down the street? The one whose mother doesn't think ADD meds are a good idea? The one who bit the cat last time he was in the house and made your daughter cry because he called her an ugly poopyhead? You don't have to let him come over. You don't have to say why, either.

Fourth Amendment: Prohibition Of Unreasonable Searches And Seizure

Despite the sticky fingerprints on every single thing in your house, you do in fact have the right to have your own stuff, and you are absolutely allowed to go ballistic if you find pink Build-a-Bear fur stuck in the brush of your new $20.00 mascara.

Fifth Amendment: You Have The Right To Remain Silent

No, when you've just finished a ten hour work day only to come home and put a load of wash in the machine, you don't have to answer the forty billion questions about where a rainbow goes. More to the point, you have the right to be IN silence for at least as long as it takes you to go to the bathroom one time a day *de minimus.*

Sixth Amendment: Right To A Speedy Trial And To Confront Witnesses

Parents are all about swift justice, and confronting witnesses. Confronting them with the fact that every last one of them will be in trouble if they don't give up the perpetrator? That's totally fair.

Seventh Amendment: Right To A Trial By Jury

The problem with a right to a trial by jury is that it ensures that you get a jury of your peers. You are Wonder Woman. You have no peers. It is lonely at the top. Lucky for your kids, you were once like them, so you can act as judge, jury, AND executioner, thus helping along that speedy trial thing in Amendment Six. In any event, if/when you completely lose it, odds are there will be at least one parent on your jury, and it only takes one juror to prevent a conviction.

Eighth Amendment: No Cruel And Unusual Punishments

You can't mete out cruel AND unusual punishments. But here's a secret -- they can be cruel OR unusual. Besides, sometimes cruel is in the eye of the beholder. My daughter would tell you that six hours without access to Apple products is cruel. I might disagree. As for unusual? I applaud the creativity of certain parents on the internet.

Ninth Amendment: This Isn't All

In the real Constitution, the 9th Amendment says something like, "just because we didn't say it here doesn't mean it doesn't exist as a right somewhere else." I think this gives us the right to claim limitless authority and change our minds with impunity. It's a little bit of a stretch, but the stretch marks on your belly prove that stretching is sometimes a good thing.

Tenth Amendment: Anything That Isn't A Federal Power Goes To The State

This means that if you are tired and simply don't feel like dealing with it, you can tell your kids to go ask Dad. Or Grandma. Or the shady looking guy blowing the leaves off the neighbor's lawn. No matter how much of an authority you are, you can always pass the buck. We'll call it delegation, because that sounds better than shirking.

Now. If you'll excuse me, I've got some rights that need enforcing.

False Modesty

Because I am not the biggest fan of premature dying, I tend to go to the doctor rather often. My family's health history is not exactly robust, with very few of us making it past our early 70s, and quite a few dipping out before then. Of course, the generations old enough to be in those categories all began smoking in their early teens and most of them took their last puff along with their last breath, so a lot of it may have something to do with that, but still. Heart disease, cancer, diabetes, crippling arthritis, and relatively harmless but very annoying tremors abound.

So I like to get checked out.

This morning, I went for my annual gynecological check up. A friend's daughter, who is half my age and otherwise extremely healthy and perfect in every way, recently had to have some disturbing cells removed from her nether regions, so I felt Righteous and On Top Of Things getting checked out while I had no symptoms.

My groinocologist (as my Dad would say) is a nice, friendly guy who was recommended to me by a friend. Recommended to me so highly, in fact, that I told her that according to the laws of the state of Georgia, being so satisfied with one's doctor can be considered adultery in a court of law. (This is not true, in case you were wondering. When in doubt, do NOT take me seriously.)

Anyhoo, I got there, did my obligatory sit in the waiting room, and then was ushered back by a nurse, who made me stand on the scale. I hate this, because it reminds me of every Oreo I've eaten in times of trouble and every piece of birthday cake I ate with gusto because I felt like it was a sin to turn it down. I'm always tempted to take off my shoes and everything that is decent to take off in a hallway, but I never do. Because maybe I can convince myself later that I don't really weigh that much, since my shoes weight twenty pounds each.

After officially registering as enormous on the scale (muscle weighs more than fat, right?) I was taken into an exam room, where the doctor came in and talked to me about updates to my medical history, etc. He then handed me a gown and a paper sheet and told me to put the gown on with the opening in the front, and the sheet would drape over my waist. He then left the room so I could undress. Which is typical, but also fairly insane. I am paying him good money to manhandle my lady parts and make sure that none of them are diseased. I know good and well that in a few minutes he is not only going to touch me in intimate ways, but with a halogen light shining on all my glory so he can see the details. But he can't watch me take off my pants?

I've given birth enough times with doctors and nurses and orderlies and cleaning staff and various and sundry other people in the room so as to be unable to count the number of people who were in the room. Afterwards, naked and exhausted, I let a very insistent Jamaican woman touch my breasts in a thousand ways to try to teach me how to get my son to get some nourishment. While lunch was being delivered and people were coming to visit.

So I'm not very shy about my body anymore. I know that medical professionals are professionals and aren't thinking, as my son would, "Boobies!" Instead, they're thinking, "Oh, Lord, these things are enormous. It is going to take me for-freaking-ever to examine them thoroughly, and I was hoping to go to lunch sometime today." I'm just a patient in a long day of patients. My body is special to me and (I hope) to my husband, but everyone else on the planet could do without seeing more of it than is absolutely necessary. Why do I have to put on the silly robe thing that opens in the front just so you can open it and touch the parts it is allegedly covering? Why do I bother using this giant sized paper towel to cover my nakedness like a fig leaf when it is going to be thrown to the side and my feet put in stirrups in five minutes? I mean, I wouldn't expose anything in the Kroger, but this is a doctor. Seems like a whole lot of false and wasted modesty to me.

Then there's the chitchat. Like I said, my doctor is a very nice, personable guy, and we have similar backgrounds and views on the universe, at least as much as I can tell from talking to him through the gap in my knees as he does his job. There is nothing odd or awkward or, even, particularly special about the conversation: it could be had at any cocktail party or business networking event, except for where his hands are. If I think about it too much it feels weird. So I just separate my head from my body and let my mouth do the talking.

Which is probably a good thing. If some other part started talking, I'd need a doctor of another kind.

Ode to the Marching Band

This is fall and this is the deepest part of the deep south, and that means that it is football season. People only get a little excited around here about pro football, but love of a college team will forge (or break) friendships, and Friday night means heading out to the local high school stadium, whether or not you have a kid that goes to the high school, or you went to that high school, or have any connection to that high school beyond a geographic location.

To me, however, and to many other kids, past, present, and future, the fall will always mean marching season. No, this blog is not an ode to the heroes who get sung at every pep rally and school dance. This is an ode to the unsung heroes, the ones who actually do and prompt the singing: the marching band.

Let me announce my marching band creds: I marched in high school and in college. In high school, I marched because if you wanted to be in the concert band, which I did, you had to march. In college, I marched because, as a student at Duke University during the glory days of Christian Laettner and Bobby Hurley and Grant Hill, I wanted front row seats to every basketball game, and you couldn't be in the pep band without being in the marching band. I never particularly liked marching. But I liked playing with a band, and my marching band friends are still my friends to this day.

Make no bones about it, marching is work. Make fun of that tuba player, why don't you, and while you're at it, lift that enormous metal thing heating up in the sun, and carry it around while playing memorized music and moving in precise maneuvers that, if done incorrectly, could result in a truly embarrassing and YouTube worthy pile of humanity and musical instruments. Now do it while wearing a polyester thermos-like uniform (keeps the hot things hot and the cool things cool!) and a hat with a giant feather sticking out of it.

These kids work hard, a lot harder than I did in my day. Marching band camp is grueling 12 hour days full of non-stop movement. Practices are out in the Georgia August heat in the worst part of the day. The field is assigned to the 'real' athletes during the time when the sun isn't directly overhead and when it hasn't spent a whole day making the asphalt into the LaBrea Tar Pit Parking Lot. The only time the band can practice without interrupting anyone else is under a blazing sun that has already worn out its welcome.

I get that people are there for the game. I get that parts of the game make you want to stand up and scream, and that the suspense of the game is the fun of it all. I get that you don't want to run to the snack bar for nachos with plastic cheese and a snout-and-entrail laden hot dog during the game because you might miss something huge. You can't pause live games, and there won't be seventy jillion replays like there are on tv. It won't come up later on ESPN. That huge interception, that touchdown run, that miracle catch – if you don't see it live, you ain't going to see it. So I get why you save your potty breaks and snack breaks during the breaks in football. I get that you wouldn't be there at all if it were just a marching band showcase.

Just remember. Those student athletes with the shoulder pads aren't the only ones out there performing. The band worked hard to bring you that halftime show. Pay attention to it, even if it is just out of politeness. Clap for them. Cheer for them. Say 'good job' to the kid carrying a saxophone out of the stands at the end of the game even if you didn't actually pay attention to him playing. He won't know. He'll just hear the compliment.

And when you hear that drum line echoing off the stands, know that's the sound of the Little Drummer Boys (and girls) proclaiming the gifts of football season.

We All Get Lit

It is the holiday season, and as a Jew living in a predominantly Christian neighborhood, it can be a little lonely. My holiday isn't represented in the local retail stores, at the schools, or, well, pretty much anywhere that I didn't personally provide the materials for it to be represented. Our house is the dark, mean looking one without lights or a tree.

Don't get me wrong – I'm not saying that I don't appreciate the quiet(er) beauty of the holiday I celebrate in December, or that the stores should change their merchandise to suit the pleasure of a handful of customers. It's just a little different looking at all this community festiveness as an outsider.

That said, I'm actually kind of glad I don't have to deal with all of that. I mean, I really do enjoy looking at other people's Christmas trees. I could spend hours looking at all the ornaments and smelling the pine. But the thought of having that in my house? I know for an absolute fact that I would be the person who keeps their tree up until sometime in April because I just don't have the wherewithal to take it all down.

I'm nothing short of awed with people who manage to transform their homes into decorated showcases all for the celebration of one day. I can't keep the stuff on my shelves visible under layers of dust and papers that have somehow landed on top. There is no way I could carefully pack all that away every year and replace it with a cute little mouse village that lights up, much less reverse the process at the end of the holiday season.

I do like driving around and looking at the lights people put up, and marvel that the ability to do these things is within the grasp of people I know. Regular, ordinary, everyday people manage to put up a string of lights in a straight line along their garage. It's a holiday miracle! In my house, we're lucky to get the gutters cleaned out every few years or so. There's no way we could decorate them or make them twinkle.

I do buy presents for my kids, at least eight apiece, one for each night, thought with grandma and aunts, etc., they usually get more than that. I don't have a tree to put them under, so I usually store them in my office until a week before, then shove them in a corner of the living room. It is not quite as festive looking as under the tree, but I can promise you that my kids like getting stuff whether or not pine sap has dripped on it. Of course, if I personally have wrapped the presents, they just look like wadded up balls of wrapping paper with some tape stuck randomly all over them, making the corner look like a trash pile, but hey – the kids still get gifts, and it's all about the stuff, right?

No. No, it isn't. Whether you are celebrating the birth of Christ, the miracle of the oil lamp after a Maccabee victory, Festivus, Diwali, another holiday, or simply enjoying that special holiday feeling you get when the weather is cooler and everything is twinkly, we all have our own kind of lights to light. We all get lit one way or another. It is all about a shared experience with family and friends.

That experience I'm talking about?

That would be egg nog.

Balls in the Air

If you believe the little number next to the word "Inbox," as of this writing, I have 3,982 unread emails in my inbox. In one of my accounts. One of them just says, "9,999+." At any given moment, I have about five active email accounts, each used for different purposes, and each of which has to be checked semi-regularly lest something get by me.

Needless to say, stuff gets by me all the time. I check my work email a lot more closely than I check my spammy email account (which used to be my main account, so people who are allergic to changing my email in their contacts still send me stuff there.) As a result, things that are actually important don't get by me often, but what I think is actually important and what the sender thinks is actually important are often completely unrelated things. I mean, every single thing someone wants to tell me is important on some level, but we have to be honest and admit that some things are on fire and need to be doused immediately, and some things are more of a small, controlled burn, or maybe just a little bit warmer than room temperature, and can wait until tomorrow. Or next week.

I have a lengthy, numbered to-do list that I keep on my desk. When something new comes up that isn't actively flaming, I put it on the bottom of the list. If it is a new thing that is afire and threatens to burn down everything else, then I put it on a special emergency list that gets done first.

Each week I rewrite the list, and re-prioritize what goes on top. Nothing comes off the list until it is done. Some things (like: check email) are repeated on the list because they have to be done again and again and again. For example, in the time it took me to type just this much, seven heretofore unseen emails popped into my inbox. Five of them appear to be spam: one is just normal correspondence, and one may or may not be flammable. This, of course, does not count Facebook and Twitter and Linked In notifications and private messages. And the four other email accounts.

If the thing is on my List (and here I will begin to capitalize the word to emphasize that this is no ordinary list like a grocery list or a bucket list or list of Academy Award Nominees) it will get done. It may be a good long while, but I promise you it will not be forgotten. If it is not on my list, chances are dicey. Sometimes I will wake up at 3:00 a.m. with the sudden realization that something that is about to catch fire is not on the List and I will have to send myself an email to remind myself to put the item on my List before I can try to go back to sleep. Which doesn't always work, because I know that sometimes emails get by me, too. So I'll repeat it to myself (emailLisaemailLisaemailLisaemailLisae-mailLisa) in the hopes that I might spontaneously remember, which is about half as likely as actually getting the email.

I feel badly for people, often kindly, deserving people, whose related tasks don't ever seem to get near the top of the list either because they are quiet or the task is relatively unimportant, even though they aren't. For example, I had the privilege of going to college with the talented sports writer Beau Dure. He wrote a book about women's soccer called "Enduring Spirit: Restoring Professional Women's Soccer to Washington" that I wanted an autographed copy of to give to one of my son's friends for her birthday. I bought the book on Amazon, had it shipped to him, and then he shipped it to me, with my promise that I would reimburse him the shipping. "pay Beau" has been on my List since late April. I actually paid Beau yesterday, which was July 20th. Beau is a nice guy. Beau is a talented guy. Beau deserved his six bucks plus interest a long long time ago. He didn't deserve to wait, but he did. I'm sorry it took me so long, Beau, and I'm hoping that this unsolicited plug for your book will help make up for it in some small way.

Keeping track of things is difficult. Between my three jobs, my two and a half children, and things for my own self (like – do something about that unibrow before I scare little children in the streets or get mistakenly deported to Russia) there's a lot of balls in the air, and some of them are going to be dropped. These days I feel like I start most conversations with, "I'm sorry it took me so long to get back to you."

So, if you are one of the balls in the air waiting to be caught, I'm sorry you're just dangling there like something out of the Matrix. I know I shouldn't have thrown so many balls up there, but I did, and there's no going back now. I can't unthrow that ball. It is no reflection on you, or your importance in my life, or whether or not you matter in the grand scheme of things. It's just that some of those balls are grenades, and I have to deal with those first, lest there be civilian casualties.

Really. It's all about the safety of the children. Or maybe who is yelling at me the loudest. Something like that.

ACKNOWLEDGEMENTS

As anyone who has written a book will tell you, the writing part is the easy part. The hard part is editing, polishing, tearing out great chunks of your (literary) baby, and, of course, getting anyone to read it. Shouting to an empty room is the nightmare of every writer.

So I owe a word of thanks to everyone who made sure my room was not empty.

Thank you to my family, for letting themselves be the subject of nearly every essay in here. Thank you especially to my children, the Dufflets, who are at an age now that they could easily freak out and refuse to allow me to use their stories. I am known as EmbarrassingDuffMom on Instagram because, well, why pretend? The fact that my children have not yet melted into the carpet in teenage humiliation is a miracle.

Thank you to all my friends who are still willing to spend time with me despite my oversharing.

Thank you to all the amazing writers who agreed to have their names associated with this book and even printed on the back cover: Mary Patterson Thornburg, Heather J. McAdams, Gianetta Palmer, Keith Stewart, Stephanie D. Lewis, Allia Zobel Nolan, and Elaine Ambrose. I promise you I have threatened none of them with bodily harm. If you haven't read their books yet, you should. I'll wait while you order them all on Amazon or your online retailer of choice.

Thank you especially to Mary Patterson Thornburg and Heather J. McAdams for their nit-picky (I swear! This is a compliment!) editing styles and thematic help. The book is more readable, and makes more sense because of their input. (Once again – have you read their books yet? No? What are you waiting for?)

Thank you to everyone I met at or through the Erma Bombeck Writers Workshop. A more supportive group of writers you will never find. I think of my writing career as "before" and "after" Erma. Ermites make me feel legit.

Thank you to Suzen Pettit and Michelle Kulp, marketing experts extraordinaire, who are the only reason that anyone that isn't my family has read anything I've ever written.

As always, thank you to my Southern Baptist conscience, Diane Hale. This is something every New York Jew needs.

Thank you in a million ways to Sharon Swanepoel, without whose call in 2012 for Patch bloggers, I probably wouldn't have started down this journey. She started me off, and her encouragement along the way is invaluable. If you want to thank her, you'll go to www.monroelocal.org and sign up for everything. It's also the only place you'll find my award winning "Legalese" column, unless by the time this is published it has been syndicated and found in newspapers everywhere.

Thank you to the Jew Crew for not seeming to mind when I say things I would never put in print.

Thank you to Saifur Rahman (iamsaifurrahman on Fiverr) for designing the awesome cover, and to Phanduy (also on Fiverr) for drawing the amazing caricature on the front cover, which makes me giggle every time I see it. Also, thanks to whomever programmed the MSWord spell-check, without whom I would never have been able to spell "caricature."

And, of course, thank you to you for actually reading this book and reviewing it (with as many stars as humanly possible) on line in many places. Hinntttttttttttt.

66401755R00107

Made in the USA
Charleston, SC
17 January 2017